CW01638437

The bike tore [illegible], and gradually Ker[illegible]nd. He revved up his [illegible]suddenly broke free, overtaking [illegible] ...ming up to the grids.

Kerry Hutson lived and dreamed speedway, and his great ambition was to ride for *The Barton Barons.* Years before, his father had been a speedway rider in Barton, and had risen to be a professional and an international star. Kerry's brother was now riding for the *Barons* and determined to make it into the big league.

But when Todd Edwards, his father's old enemy, returned from London, the whole tenor of Kerry's life was changed. Todd had been a small-time crook, run out of town by Kerry's father. Prosperous now, but still a crook, his vendetta against the Hutson family was waged with an intensity beyond all reason. Bribery, blackmail and kidnapping were Todd's weapons, and his accomplice carried a gun . . .

This is John Foster's first book for young people, and is based on the successful BBC 1 series.

KING CINDER

JOHN FOSTER

British Broadcasting Corporation

King Cinder, by John Foster, was first shown on BBC 1 in autumn 1977, with Peter Duncan as Kerry, Lesley Manville as Nikki, Jeremy Arnold as Trevor, Michael Hawkins as Todd, Derek Ware as Clayton and Tony Caunter as Richard Hutson. The series was directed by John Prowse and produced by Anna Home.

Published by the
British Broadcasting Corporation
35 Marylebone High Street
London W1M 4AA

ISBN 0 563 17419 6
First published 1977
© John Foster 1977

Printed in England by
Tonbridge Printers Ltd
Shipbourne Road
Tonbridge, Kent

1 Visitors

Kerry heard them first. He was lying on top of his bed, lazily flipping through some speedway magazines. Suddenly he stopped and listened. The sound was far off, coming from across the other side of town. Just a distant roar of motorbike engines along the coastline.

Kerry got up quickly and crossed to his bedroom window. He was nearly seventeen, tall, lanky, with a shock of blonde hair hanging over his forehead. He was wearing a green shirt and blue denim jeans. He looked out across the rooftops. Then he saw them. The knot of motorbike riders moved swiftly up through the town, winding along the narrow streets like a drove of bluebottle flies, the metal on their bikes glinting brightly in the morning sunlight. With their black leather outfits, weighty helmets and rubber goggles, they looked like spacemen. Kerry watched intently. They rode elegantly through Barton, yet their appearance looked threatening. The black riders were hunched over their machines, and the high-pitched whine of their engines echoed loudly along the terraced rows. Saturday-morning shoppers paused and turned to watch the gang as they swarmed past, weaving their way confidently through the busy traffic.

Kerry felt a wave of excitement run through him. The very sight of the powerful motorbikes streaking along, and the heavy, intense roar of the engines, was exhilarating. They swung into the street and tore violently down it, approaching the house.

They're coming here, Kerry thought to himself. They're back again! They're making for the restaurant.

Kerry rubbed his knuckles across his jaw. Tension rose in him as he watched the gang gather in the street below, outside the forecourt of the restaurant. Then they rode slowly, in a wide, menacing circle in the middle of the street, wheeling round and mounting the pavement on either side, revving up their motorbike engines into an ugly, deafening growl. Their tinted plastic visors, and the black silk scarfs wrapped tightly round their mouths and faces, made it impossible for anyone to identify the riders. Yet Kerry knew only too well who they were. He'd crossed their path many times before. He would recognise them anywhere. Lacey's mob, from the neighbouring town of Weyfield. And they were trouble.

Kerry crossed quickly to the door, out on to the landing. He got to the stairs, straddled the banister bar, and slid swiftly down it into the hallway. Here he paused, listening. Outside, the gang had silenced their motorbike engines and were chanting loudly together. Their voices were harsh and sarcastic: "King Cinder! King Cinder! Hip-*hooray!*"

Kerry went quickly into the living-room and peered out between the curtains. The gang were now outside the entrance of the restaurant, sitting astride their motorbikes. Some of them had removed their helmets and face scarfs. Kerry spotted Lacey among them. He was about the same age as Kerry, heavily-built, dark-haired, wearing a swanky, petulant air of aggressiveness. Fancy yourself as something, don't you, thought Kerry, as he watched Lacey whip the gang up into even greater fervour. But you're all front.

"King Cinder! *Ray! Ray! Ray!*" The gang laughed and jeered. The restaurant was called *The King Cinder*. Some years ago, Richard Hutson had been an international speedway star, and had become a legend in the town. When he retired from the track, he converted part of the large family house into a licensed restaurant, naming it after his own speedway title. It had proved a great success. People came from miles around to eat at *The King Cinder*, and the restaurant was especially popular with holiday-makers. But the years since his retirement hadn't been easy. His wife was killed in a road accident, leaving him with two young sons, to bring up single-handed. Kerry's elder brother, Trevor, had now left school and was living away from home, working in a nearby factory and riding for the local speedway team in his spare time. Kerry was in his final year at school. It was all getting better – but then, suddenly, right at the height of the tourist season, *The King Cinder* had been one of several restaurants in the town singled out for attacks of vandalism. The gang had succeeded in frightening away customers and business had fallen off badly. This was their fourth visit to the restaurant within a few weeks and nobody had known who they were or where they came from. But they had never before turned up while Kerry was at home. He should have guessed that Lacey was behind it.

Lacey ordered the others to stop chanting. They all dismounted, parked their bikes in a haphazard line at the kerb, and then slouched towards the entrance of the restaurant, their heavy boots smacking across the pavement.

Kerry tip-toed silently downstairs and hid behind the curtains which separated the restaurant from the kitchen behind it. It was lunchtime, and *The King Cinder* was busy. The tables were covered with crisp, white cloths, and on the walls hung a number of framed photographs, many of them autographed, of past speedway stars. On one wall was a mosaic of four floodlit motorbike riders, plastered with mud, roaring round a stadium speedway track. Soft music played in the background and the atmosphere was relaxed. Customers, mostly holiday-makers, chatted quietly together.

Richard Hutson was behind the bar, pouring out a lager for a customer. He was in his early forties, a big, burly man with a broad, generous face. Although he was smartly dressed in a navy-blue blazer and grey flannel trousers, he looked a bit out of place as a restaurant proprietor. He seemed somehow to be more suited to the outdoor life.

There was only one waiter, Ted, who had been with *The King Cinder* since it opened, and looked as if he had been a waiter all his working life. He was taking an order from a family of American tourists.

Suddenly the door burst open, and Lacey stood there, grinning, rubbing his leather-gloved hands together. A hushed silence fell as Lacey stepped inside, followed by the half-dozen members of his gang. The door was kicked shut with a heavy thud. Ted glanced anxiously at the pack of youths.

Lacey looked across at the bar. "Hello there, Captain!" he beamed.

Richard Hutson plonked down the glass of lager and crossed quickly between the tables towards Lacey. "About turn and on your way! I want no more trouble here!"

"Trouble, Captain?" Lacey swaggered forward, looking round impishly at the tables of silent customers. "What you talking about? *What* trouble?"

Lacey swung his arm out, casually knocking a cup and saucer off the edge of a table. The crockery fell to the floor with a loud crash. Lacey pulled a face and two of the youths giggled. "Oh, sorry Captain," said Lacey, "that was clumsy!"

Several customers at a table near the door got up and quickly left the restaurant without paying their bill. Three of the youths immediately sat down in their places and began banging their fists heavily on the table, shouting: "Service! Service!"

Kerry remained where he was, hidden and biding his time. He saw his father pace angrily up to Lacey. "I said *out*!"

Lacey then obstinately squatted down right on top of the table where the American tourists were sitting, knocking a carafe of water over on to the table-cloth. The Americans gathered up their cameras and other belongings and left hurriedly.

Other members of the gang had taken over and occupied tables, knocking crockery and cutlery to the floor. They began thumping the tables, chanting together: "Service! Service! Service!"

Richard Hutson grabbed hold of Lacey by his leather tunic and swung him off the table. "Now! Let's have it! What's behind all this?"

Lacey violently pulled himself free, sat down in one of the chairs and joined in with the others, banging his fist on the table. "Hamburger and chips!" he bellowed.

Hutson looked round. "Ted," he called briskly, "phone the police."

Ted turned to the coin-operated telephone in an alcove on the far side of the restaurant. Two members of the gang swiftly blocked his path, standing in front of him, hands on their hips, grinning. One of them pressed the palm of his hand against Ted's chest, gently pushing him back, forcing the waiter to sit down on one of the vacant chairs.

Lacey said: "Now, now, Captain! You don't need the law! You're over-reacting!"

"What's the idea? Coming here, week after week, wrecking the place?"

"Just a bit of fun, Captain, that's all!"

All the customers had now left, and the gang occupied many of the tables. Some of the youths were still banging their fists on the tables, demanding attention. Others were eating from the plates of food left by the customers. Ted remained seated, watching Lacey and the others uneasily. Broken plates, cups and saucers were scattered across the floor, and the gang were now shouting and thumping the table tops. Then they began chanting again in mindless unison: "*Ooy! Ooy! Ooy!*"

Hutson's face was flushed and he stood looking as if he might explode at any second. He didn't dare move, unable to trust his own temper.

Kerry had waited impatiently to find out what would happen. Before he made his move, he wanted first to see exactly what the gang did. But he had restrained himself long enough. Now he chose his moment, lifted back the curtain and stepped quietly out into the restaurant. Nobody noticed him, not even his father.

Kerry's voice, coming suddenly from the far end of the restaurant, was loud and hard with threat: "*Lacey!*"

The gang fell silent and sat motionless as if a spell had suddenly been cast over them. Lacey had his back to Kerry, but he recognised Kerry's voice. The truculent smirk disappeared from his face. He twisted round on the chair.

"Hutson!" Lacey spat Kerry's surname out, standing quickly, the chair scraping back behind him. His eyes grew as hard and as bright as marbles. He turned to confront Kerry, looking bent on a scrap.

Kerry moved forward. "So it's you that's been causing all the bother."

His father could see a fight coming and tried to step in. "Now stop! No more trouble—"

But he was too late. Lacey suddenly dived forward towards Kerry, attempting to grasp him round the neck. Kerry deftly side-stepped him, and stuck his foot out, tripping Lacey up as he pitched past. Then Lacey went crashing into a table, grabbing hold of the tail of the table-cloth as he tumbled to the floor, dragging the cloth off with him and sending all the crockery and cutlery flying. Kerry pounced quickly on top of Lacey, pressing his knees firmly upon Lacey's chest, holding his wrists down, pinning him to the floor.

Several members of the gang got to their feet. Lacey was trying desperately to heave Kerry off, but Kerry sat heavily upon him. Lacey struggled helplessly. "Get off, Hutson, *you*—"

Lacey twisted violently, shouting at the others: "Get him off me!"

The youths edged forward, surrounding Kerry and Lacey. But Kerry's father was there first. "Break it up!" he shouted.

Suddenly Lacey tossed Kerry off. They both rolled over between the chairs, Lacey clasping his gloved hands roughly over Kerry's face, smothering his eyes and mouth. Kerry's father reached down and grabbed them both by the scruffs of their necks, dragged them to their feet, separating them and holding them apart. "Right! Now just stop this!"

Kerry and Lacey hung apart in his grip like two puppets, still itching to get at one another, sparring in the air like boxers. The gang stood round them in a menacing circle, poised ready.

Kerry tried to pull himself free, but his father spoke sharply: "Kerry! Leave it!" Then abruptly he released them both. Stiff with anger, he violently barged his way through the surrounding youths, walking quickly towards the phone alcove. "This is a job for the police!"

Lacey suddenly grew tense, his face pinched. The gang

backed sullenly away towards the door. "Come on, Captain," said Lacey, with a new air of mateyness, "not the police. We're only having a laugh!"

But Kerry's father picked up the receiver and began dialling. "Have it somewhere else," he said.

The bell jangled as the door was pulled open and the gang began hastily crowding outside. Lacey glanced round at them, then took a few steps back past the tables. "OK, Captain, OK! We're going!"

Kerry's father looked across at Lacey. He stopped dialling, but still held the receiver in a threatening manner. "And don't come back!"

"What hospitality, hey, lads?" Lacey joked at the youths. None of them was listening. "We'll have to find somewhere else to eat our dinner."

"You do that!"

Lacey swaggered to the door. The others were outside, waiting for him in a group on the pavement. Lacey looked coldly at Kerry. "We'll meet again, Hutson."

"Like it says in the song."

"One day soon!" promised Lacey.

"Wear a clean shirt," Kerry replied.

Lacey's face flushed with anger. He turned suddenly and went out, slamming the door heavily behind him.

"Who are they, Kerry?" his father asked, replacing the receiver.

"Lacey and his mob. A gang across from Weyfield."

Ted poured himself a glass of water and sipped it slowly, his hand shaking slightly. The two chefs emerged from the kitchen and looked across at the debris-strewn interior of the restaurant. They began picking up some of the chairs.

Richard Hutson moved over to the window and Kerry followed him. They watched the gang outside strap on their helmets, mount their motorbikes, and begin revving up their engines. "This is the fourth time it's happened. They just arrive out of the blue and put the boot in. Then off they go again." He watched as the gang roared down the High Street.

"That lot are always causing bother," said Kerry.

"Other places in Barton have had the same trouble. Pubs and restaurants, some of the cafés along the promenade."

"What about the police?"

His father shrugged. "It's been reported," he said, "but nobody had a clue who they were. Could have been any gang of kids."

Kerry frowned. "Why didn't you phone through to the police just now, like you threatened?"

"Because those kids didn't hang round long enough to get caught."

Kerry thought his father sounded a bit evasive. He could have had them arrested if he really wanted to. "But now you know it's Lacey's gang, the police can go and grab them."

His father thought for a moment, then he shook his head slowly. "No," he said, "I don't want the police involved yet. I reckon there's something more to this. Those kids aren't doing it just for kicks "

"How d'you mean?" asked Kerry, surprised.

"They've been roaming around visiting places like this and smashing them up, regularly, for the past month or so . . . as if they've got it all planned out . . ."

Kerry laughed. "*What?*" he exclaimed. "Not those flea brains!" But Kerry could see that his father was in dead earnest. "Anyway, what would be the point of it all?"

"I'm not sure yet," said his father quietly, "but I reckon this has been organised."

Kerry just couldn't take any of it seriously. "Come on, Dad," he laughed. "That lot couldn't organise Christmas!"

"Somebody is. Somebody's behind it . . ."

Todd stared out through the windscreen, watching the string of motorbike riders approach the car, skirting along the outside of the traffic on the opposite side of the road. The gang teased out a path through the bottle-neck traffic jam and streamed away up the hill, along the coastal road which wound across the edge of the bay towards Weyfield.

Todd glanced casually at his watch. They had been stuck here just outside Barton for over ten minutes, right in the midst of the long queue of holiday traffic. Car horns were being honked loudly and impatiently. Some drivers climbed out of their cars and squinted along the promenade trying to determine the cause of the hold up. Two men, their cars jammed together near the middle of the road, were having a violent argument. The long, straggling line of immobile vehicles glinted brightly in the sticky sunshine.

Todd switched off the engine and sat back, took off his sunglasses and wiped them carefully with a handkerchief. Despite the intense heat and pestering flies, he looked cool and relaxed; a smart, dark-haired, sturdy man in his mid-forties. He watched the June sea cream quietly along the shore below the promenade. The stretch of beach was a maze of sun-drenched holiday-makers camped out along the sand. Deck-chair attendants weaved their way busily between family groups. A crowd of kids swarmed round an ice-cream van. Some men were fishing off the pier, which jutted out like a black finger into the sea. Surf-riders bobbed swiftly over the white-tipped waves. Motorboats purred distantly across the bay.

"Oh come on, come on!" groaned Clayton, the man sitting next to Todd in the front passenger seat. He spoke wearily and irritably, addressing the traffic through the windscreen in front of them. Both men sat in their shirt sleeves and all four windows were fully wound down. Neither of them looked like holiday-makers. They could have been businessmen, perhaps, on their way to a weekend conference.

Clayton looked sweaty, tense and bad-tempered. He was a tubby man in his late forties. "What's the hold up?" he asked, glancing at Todd.

Todd shrugged. "How do I know? We've caught the weekend trippers I suppose." Todd spoke briskly, years away from Barton, living in the city, had smoothed out his local accent.

Clayton still blustered. "A hundred-mile journey down here and then we get stuck in some traffic jam!"

"Just be patient," Todd told him.

"I want a bath and a long cool drink," bleated Clayton. Todd said nothing and carried on cleaning his sunglasses. Clayton was getting on his nerves.

Clayton wiped away the sweat prickling his bald head with a grubby handkerchief, and patted his thick, red lips. He took a sip from a tin of Coke. "What are we doing down here, anyway?" Clayton sounded as if he didn't expect an answer. He spoke tonelessly, weary of having repeated the same question many times before.

The traffic began nosing forward slowly. Todd fired the starter, put the engine into gear and the red Maxi crawled behind the queue of cars. They were moving along the promenade road, then Todd took a right turn and swung the car into an empty side street.

Clayton persisted with his questions as the car picked up speed. "What's this trip all about, Todd?" he asked. "I've got a right to know."

Todd spoke dryly, in a flat, dismissive voice. "I've told you. Wait."

The car passed along a sullen row of terraced houses. "You must have a reason for coming back to your home town after twenty years."

"Yes," said Todd quietly, "I've got a reason."

"But why all this secrecy? What are we after?"

There was a short pause. Todd was taking the car down a series of narrow back streets, short cuts which he still remembered, heading towards the town centre. "We've come to find King Cinder," he said.

Clayton frowned and almost chuckled. "King *who*?" he asked.

Todd pulled a folded newspaper cutting out of his back trouser pocket and handed it to Clayton. "A man named Richard Hutson."

Clayton unfolded the cutting and squinted down at it. The neatly trimmed newspaper was yellowed at the edges. It had a banner headline, which read: KING CINDER!! And underneath was a picture of Richard Hutson, sitting astride a motorbike, dressed in speedway gear. He was holding a huge prize cup above his head and grinning broadly. "Richard Hutson," read Clayton, "home-grown speedway star . . ."

"*Ex* speedway star," corrected Todd.

Clayton glanced down at the date of the newspaper cutting.

It was over ten years old. "Famous in his day," Todd added. "Rode for England in the World Championships."

Clayton handed the cutting back. "So you know this bloke Hutson, then?"

"From way back." Todd's voice was cold.

"Old mates?" Todd shook his head, smiling. Clayton grinned. "Old enemies, then?" he asked hopefully.

Todd watched silently through the windscreen as they drove along. He swerved to avoid a crowd of kids playing ball in the street. The town hadn't changed much. The same dead-end granite rows. The squat little corner shops. The bed-and-breakfast houses dotted along the streets near the sea-front. The docks in the distance with their black cranes and machinery looking like squashed spiders. The jerry-built bus station. The lonely hilltop cemetery where Todd's parents lay buried. The cat walks and market square.

The car glided past the secondary school Todd went to when he was a kid. There were still the rusty iron railings and the flat stretch of tarmac, the grey collection of school buildings beyond. Todd recalled the smell of chalk dust and boiled cabbage along the corridors. The town hall clock struck two tinny notes nearby. Everything looked familiar, perhaps a bit smaller and tidier in appearance than he remembered it. *Sticksville,* thought Todd.

Clayton had grown impatient. "So, come on, Todd. What's behind it all?"

"How many times do I have to say it? *Wait!*"

"Why come all the way from London to look up some has-been speedway star?"

"Because!" Todd snapped.

Clayton persisted. "What do you want of him, this 'King Cinder'?"

Todd lit a small cigar. "You will find out very shortly."

Clayton finally lost his temper. "Streuth!" he exploded. He chucked the Coke tin out of the car window. It clattered noisily across the pavement.

Todd glanced at Clayton. "Calm down, Clayton," he said. "You'll see some fireworks soon enough."

"I can't wait," Clayton replied sarcastically.

Clayton wrenched open the glove compartment. Inside lay a fat bar of milk chocolate. A large pair of field glasses. And sitting there beside them was a big automatic pistol, black and shining.

Clayton snatched out the bar of chocolate and slammed the compartment shut. He broke off a piece of chocolate and bit into it. Then he sat back and looked out at the passing streets, a sulky, hound-dog expression on his face.

Maybe I should open up a bit, Todd wondered, tell Clayton more. It would be unwise to upset Clayton, especially at this stage. Clayton was an oaf, but not without his value. When it came to executing the more unpleasant tasks, he needed Clayton, a zombie with plenty of muscle. So play it crafty, Todd decided, humour him for the moment. But don't tell him too much yet. Wait till he's in it too deep.

"I'll show you where the King lives," said Todd, with a sudden air of friendliness. "He owns a restaurant."

Clayton was still sulking. "Fantastic," he sneered.

"Tonight we'll pay him a visit." Todd blew out a plume of blue cigar smoke. "But first we must have a word with our friend Lacey."

2 The Barons

Saturday was Kerry's favourite day. To begin with, there was no school, so you could have a good lie-in if you wanted. Yet even during the holidays, Kerry really looked forward to Saturday. There was something special about it, a kind of happy-go-lucky, festival feeling – particularly on Saturday nights, when there was always plenty going on. Kerry nearly always went out on Saturday night. He couldn't bear to miss out on anything and if he was forced to stay at home for some reason, he got broody and irritable, his feet began getting itchy. And the weekend was the time he saw most of Nikki, his girlfriend. It's true that he saw her on other days of the week as well, because they both went to the same Comprehensive. But that was different. Being together at school didn't really count. The teachers treated them as if they were still just clueless kids. And the others would snigger and make snide remarks when they saw Kerry and Nikki together in the playground. Sometimes it got a bit embarrassing. Alone at weekends, they felt more grown-up. They could be themselves, and do more or less what they wanted. Then it was good being together.

Saturday was special for other reasons. In the afternoon, the local speedway team, *The Barons*, had a practice run in preparation for the forthcoming race meeting at Barton Stadium. The practice track was part of a large community sportsground near the civic centre and the team members rode there most evenings and weekends. There was always a fairly relaxed atmosphere and Kerry liked to watch them riding. Often he got the chance of a race with one of the riders – usually Tom, who was a mate of Kerry's older brother, Trevor. Kerry was fanatical about speedway and an avid supporter of *The Barons*. Dad had begun his speedway career as a rider for the local team, and then become its captain. He brought fame to Barton, and it launched dad into national and international racing, as a professional. Now Trevor was riding for *The Barons*, with the intention of chucking in his job and becoming a fully fledged professional as soon as he could make it. Kerry was all set to follow suit. It was a tough life, speedway racing, but Kerry felt it in his blood. The Hutsons were a speedway family.

Apart from the chance of the occasional race down at the practice track, Kerry had also found himself a part-time job as a wall-of-death rider at the local fairground. It was only for a few evenings a week, including Saturdays, but it gave him the chance to practise motorbike riding. The fairground provided him with a special motorbike, sleek and gleaming red, with which to ride the wall-of-death. Although Kerry preferred his own motorbike, it was good to use a different, more sophisticated machine. He felt like a real dare-devil rider when he roared round the wall-of-death on that red monster! But as soon as he left school, Kerry wanted to ride for *The Barons* if he was good enough and if they would have him. Still, riding the wall-of-death took some skill and he got a great kick out of doing it. And Nikki always came to watch him ride at the fairground on Saturday night. Then, afterwards, they would go off together down the disco.

After lunch on Saturdays, Kerry usually spent a couple of hours in the garage tinkering with his motorbike – checking it over, cleaning the parts, giving it a good overhaul. He liked to get the bike in tip-top condition before he went out to the practice track. It was good fun messing about, taking the bike to bits, fiddling round with it. Kerry was dressed in a pair of old overalls, his face and hands smeared with oil. The motorbike was upside down in the middle of the garage floor. The door was slightly ajar, letting in a stream of sunlight. Kerry sat on his haunches as he worked, whistling to the tune of a pop song playing on the transistor radio beside him.

He heard footsteps smacking across the yard outside. "Kerry," his father called, "your tea's ready."

"Ta . . . just coming . . ."

Kerry's father pushed open the garage door and stepped in. He grinned when he saw Kerry in his overalls, plastered with grease. "You're in a right state!"

Kerry stood, wiping his hands with a rag. "I've just finished . . . won't take a sec. to clean up."

"Are you working down the fairground tonight?"

"Yeah!" Kerry said cheerfully. "Quick little spin round the wall-of-death!"

"Bit of extra money for you."

"Right," said Kerry, "and I get a lot out of it as well. Y'know, pitching round that wall. The crowds all stood there watching. Feels good." Kerry looked up and gave an impish grin. "Impresses the birds, too!"

"I'll bet!" laughed his father.

"Not like the real thing – but it's something till I can start speedway racing."

"Dead set on speedway, aren't you?" said his father, quietly.

"Not half!" said Kerry. "Soon as I get my chance."

"Fair enough. But concentrate on finding yourself a secure job first when you leave school."

Kerry shrugged. "I'm not bothered what job I do, so long as there's plenty of free time for racing."

But his father had grown serious, and spoke with a practical, business-like air. "*No,*" he stressed, "follow Trevor's example. Get yourself something steady."

"Trevor's only working there in that factory till he can take up racing full time."

"Kerry, you know what I think about it. Racing part-time in local speedway – fine. But getting into it professionally, that's a dodgy business."

Kerry began pulling off his overalls. "It's what we both want to do Dad, Trev and me. Ride the track as professionals, just like you did."

Kerry knew what his father was going to say next almost

word for word. He'd heard this lecture many times before. "... battling through to the top league – it can ruin your life, believe me. I've seen it happen, many a time."

"You've got to take risks if you're going to make through."

His father shook his head. "Well, it's your life," he said. "But I'd rather see both you and Trevor settled down, in regular jobs, get yourself a home and family."

"What, play it safe? Not me!"

His father just stared at Kerry for a moment. Then his face broke into a smile and he shrugged: "I don't know – kids never listen! Everything looks easy when you're young. You'll soon learn."

Kerry could never understand why his father took this attitude. It was almost as though there were more to what he said than he would ever admit. "But *you* made it, Dad!" Kerry said. "World Champion, became a legend, people still call you 'King Cinder'."

"I was lucky," said his father, quietly.

Kerry grinned. "Hey, not scared of getting upstaged, are you?"

His father did a double-take. "*What?*" He was smiling broadly, more relaxed now. His earnest, dogged manner had gone. Kerry knew that he liked having his leg pulled. "Want to keep that crown all to yourself?"

Dad punched Kerry playfully in the stomach. "Come on, numbskull," he said, "or your tea will stew till it's black!"

But there was an air of friction between Kerry and his father whenever the subject of speedway came up. He didn't even approve of Trevor riding for *The Barons* in his spare time, and there had been a bust up between them over it – that's why Trevor had left home.

Kerry missed having a brother around. "Dad," he asked quietly, "why don't you come and watch Trevor race sometimes?"

His father was silent for a moment. Then he spoke tonelessly. "Trevor doesn't want me there. I just crowd him. You know how it is."

"Never comes round here to visit you, does he?"

His father obviously didn't want to discuss it. "We don't really see eye to eye," he said.

"Seems daft, that's all. Mum's gone, there's just the three of us. Pity we can't hit it off better."

"Wish things were different," said his father, "but there it is. Trevor wants to lead his own life."

Kerry gulped down two large cups of brown tea, some cheese sandwiches, and a thick slice of saffron cake. He was reading some speedway magazines spread out on the kitchen table as he ate his tea. "How d'you rate Jeff Fuller, Dad?"

His father was sitting in an armchair, reading the newspaper. "Not a bad rider when he gets on with it. Got a lot to say for himself, though, that's his only trouble. Too much talk."

"He's in the British finals at Coventry next month," said Kerry, turning the page.

His father put down the newspaper. "Kerry, what do you know about those characters who came busting into the restaurant this morning?"

Kerry shrugged. "Just a bunch of yobs, that's all. They're always round and about, mixing it. Usually down at the speedway on Sunday afternoon when there's a meeting, looking for trouble."

"Because I reckon there's somebody behind those kids. They're just mugs – but there's someone else pulling the strings."

"Come again?"

"That crew haven't come visiting each week specially because they fancy doing my place over," said his father. "Like I said before, the same thing's happened elsewhere in town. A regular pattern."

Kerry chuckled. "What, organised crime here in Barton?"

His father stood up from the armchair and paced slowly round the room, sucking his pipe. "Business has gone down since it started, right at the height of the holiday season. It's all too much of a coincidence. There's a scheme behind it somewhere . . ."

"What do the police say?"

"They haven't got a clue. The police around here are about as sleepy as doctored tom cats!"

"So, what are you going to do?" Kerry asked.

Kerry watched his father stroll across to the window and stare outside, blowing tobacco smoke against the window pane. "Have a quiet word round town," he said. "Se what I can find out through the old grapevine. Make a few discreet enquiries . . ."

Kerry got up from the table, grinning to himself. He looked across at his father, who was standing there at the window, puffing away at his pipe, brooding over the puzzle like a master detective. "Hey, Dad . . . want to borrow my Sherlock Holmes pipe?"

Kerry pulled on his leather jacket, then strapped on his crash helmet. "Have a good night," said his father, as Kerry wheeled his motorbike out.

"Thanks . . ." Kerry mounted the motorbike and sat astride it. "I'm going over to the practice track first, see how Trevor's making out."

His father was silent for a moment. Then he said: "Well, wish him all the best."

"Okay. See y'Dad." And Kerry kicked the starting pedal. The engine spluttered into life. Kerry roared off out of the yard, and down the narrow tarmac lane at the back of the house.

Saturday afternoon traffic was busy in the High Street and Kerry sat poised on his bike, waiting for the chance to nose his way out. He didn't notice the red Maxi parked on the far side of the street, directly opposite the forecourt of *The King Cinder*.

Todd nodded towards the restaurant. "There it is, *The King Cinder*. That's were we'll find Hutson."

"Is there a queen in residence as well?" Clayton asked sarcastically.

Todd's tone was matter-of-fact. "No. Hutson's wife died years back." Then Todd noticed Kerry nursing his motorbike into the heavy stream of traffic. He pointed. "That'll be one of his sons. Kerry – he lives there with his old man."

They watched Kerry roar off down the High Street, weaving his way skilfully through the traffic. "The Crown Prince!" Clayton remarked.

"There's an older brother as well, Trevor. Lives in a bed-sitter in the town. He rides for *The Barons*."

Clayton frowned. "The *what?*"

"*The Barton Barons*. What the local speedway team call themselves."

Clayton didn't look a lot wiser, but he decided not to press the point. "What time are we meant to be meeting this kid Lacey?" he asked.

"Four o'clock."

"Then we'll be late."

Todd fired the car engine and put the vehicle into gear. "Lacey will wait," he said quietly.

Nikki lived over on Kitchener, a large, sprawling council estate on the north side of the town. Kerry rode past the rows of red-bricked, uniform bungalows and houses, down along the sinister avenues of camel-necked concrete lamp standards. Kitchener was a satellite estate and its impersonal, modernistic appearance always reminded Kerry of what he imagined a moon-base colony might look like. Yet today the sun was shining, people were out in their gardens or washing down their cars in the road outside, bringing some life to the desolate rows. A crowd of kids were playing around the rusted skeleton of an old car left abandoned on a patch of waste ground. An ice-cream van moved slowly down the row, playing *Oranges and Lemons* in a sequence of flat, metallic notes. Kerry rode on past some allotments towards the far side of the estate.

Kerry thought about Nikki as he rode along. They had been going out steadily for – how long? Well, it was over six months now. Kerry liked Nikki a lot, though he wasn't over the moon about her. That's what was good about things between them – none of this intense, heavy-breathing stuff some kids went in for. Kerry grinned to himself. Nikki would never allow that kind of thing anyway – she'd run a hundred miles if Kerry got sloppy and earnest over her. But they always had a good time together, there was plenty to laugh about. It's true that Nikki didn't rate speedway, but then you can't have everything.

Kerry turned into the road and approached the bungalow where Nikki lived. A few yards away, Kerry began honking loudly on his horn. He pulled up, switched off the engine, pushed up the visor of his helmet, and looked towards the back door of the bungalow. Eventually, Nikki emerged, frowning. She was wearing a red T-shirt, blue denims and sandals. She ran down the path, strode across the pavement up to Kerry, and stood there in front of him with her hands on her hips.

"I thought it was you," she said, "making that racket!"

"Thanks for the welcome!"

Nikki stood there, thin and pert, her head cocked to one side. "But you said tonight – meet down the fairground tonight."

"Yeah," said Kerry, "just thought I'd look by."

Nikki pretended to be cross. "You've woken up the baby – honking on that horn of yours!"

Kerry didn't believe a word of it. "Have I really?" he asked with a smile.

Nikki suddenly began laughing, tossing back her long, brown hair. She looked Kerry up and down as he sat there, astride his motorbike. "*You*!" she giggled.

"What's funny?"

"Just look at you!"

Kerry frowned. "*What?*"

"Dig me!" laughed Nikki. "I'm a speedway rider!"

"Ha *ha!*" said Kerry, petulantly.

"All set for Brands Hatch, then?"

"That's *motor* racing, twit!"

Nikki shrugged. "Same sort of thing. Blokes riding round and round in circles getting nowhere fast."

Kerry said nothing, just sat there, his shoulders hunched up, pouting his lips like a small boy.

Nikki cleared her throat. "No, seriously . . ." she said, "only joking. You look really good, just the job, honestly!" But then she broke into another giggle.

Kerry glared at her. "Thanks!" he said.

Nikki decided to change the subject. "Coming in for a cup of coffee?"

Kerry shook his head. "On my way down to the practice track, see how Trev's making out. Want to come?"

Nikki shook her head. "Mum and Dad have gone down to the beach, so I'm baby-sitting. Would do otherwise."

Kerry pushed down the visor of his helmet. "OK, see you tonight?"

"Yeah, I'll be there about eight."

"I'm dare-devil riding again tonight."

"Well, watch yourself!" said Nikki.

Kerry pushed down his foot on the starting-pedal. "I'll be all right." He glanced across at Nikki. "Hey, did I really wake up the baby?"

Nikki gave a wry smile. "No, you went and woke *me* up, didn't you?" she laughed.

"Well, I'm really sorry about that, Nikki," he said as he moved out into the road, "because with a face like yours you need as much of the old beauty sleep you can get!"

Kerry rode quickly away from the kerb. Nikki chased after him until the motorbike gathered speed and she was left standing at the kerb, waving a fist and laughing.

Kerry spun his motorbike violently round the outer edge of the track, sending up an explosion of cinder as the wheels skidded across the surface, the dust billowing thickly over him. As he roared along the broad base of the practice track, he caught a momentary glimpse through his visor of the people standing around the perimeter, watching. The nearby outbuildings across the sportsfield whirled past. The track before him seemed to rise up and race towards him as he pitched along. His blood raced, and his whole body, poised over the machine, pounded with exhilaration. The bike bounced clumsily along over the pot-holed track, but Kerry felt as if he were gliding through outer space as he swished quickly along. He was intoxicated with excitement. He was now almost level with Tom, who rode steadily along on the inside of the track.

"*Wow!*" Kerry let out a wild, spirited whoop as both riders took a corner with a skid and almost collided. Then both motorbikes burst along the track. Tom and Kerry were now level pegging.

Kerry looked across the track at Tom and bawled at him: "I'll get you on the next bend – see if I don't!" Tom glanced round, grinning at Kerry through the fog of swirling cinder ash, and began revving up his engine. "Just wait for it!" Kerry shouted, over the deafening roar.

Kerry ground the bike forward, hurling every muscle in his body behind it, willing the machine to move faster. The bike tore along the track like a jet across a skyline, and gradually inched past Tom, growling loudly towards the final bend. Kerry revved up his engine for the finishing spurt and suddenly broke free of Tom, overtaking him and wheeling towards the makeshift grids. As Kerry pitched round the final bend and roared past the grids, he threw up his arms in the air and let out a huge victory shout. Then he gripped the handlebars and swung the bike over to the side of the track, dismounted, kicked down the parking stand, leaving the bike on the grass verge.

Somebody nearby shouted: "Good racing, kid!" Kerry glanced round, grinning, as he unstrapped his helmet. He looked across the track for his brother, Trevor, who had been watching the race. At first, Kerry couldn't spot him. Then he saw him on the far side of the track. Trevor's back was turned away as he talked to another rider.

Tom bounced on to the verge, bringing his motorbike to a halt just beside Kerry. He pushed up his visor and grinned. "Well done there, Kerry!"

"Thanks for the race, Tom."

Tom removed his helmet, wiped sweat from his face, and ran his fingers through his sandy hair. "You're welcome, Kerry," he said, "it was a pretty good spin."

"Yeah!" Kerry's body was still tingling with the excitement of the race.

"You're a Hutson right enough," Tom said, smiling. "You rode that track like the bike was part of you!"

Kerry found it impossible to conceal a pleased, enthusiastic grin. And what Tom said wasn't false flattery – Kerry knew it was true. Kerry got on well with Tom. He was always the same, friendly and good humoured. He was about the same age as Trevor, twenty, fresh-faced, very much the local lad. Kerry could imagine Tom living in Barton for the rest of his life, settling down, having a family, acquiring a mortgage and a middle-aged spread. Tom was straightforward and modest about his own abilities. He simply liked speedway racing. And he was a good rider for *The Barons*.

They both walked around the perimeter of the track towards Trevor. Team riders of *The Barons* were dotted along the verge, sitting on their haunches, talking, or lying on the cropped grass. Others stood in groups, sipping from tins of Coke. All the riders were, dressed like Tom and Trevor, in the colours of *The Barons*. One day, Kerry promised himself, *I'll* be wearing those colours – one day soon.

Two of the riders mounted their motorbikes, roared on to the practice track and began racing. Kerry watched as he walked along. Then he looked out beyond the practice track across the community sportsground. A group of middle-aged men were playing cricket on a narrow strip of green grass. The gentle knock of tennis balls echoed from the tarmac courts. The blue round disc of the swimming pool dazzled in the afternoon sun as young children splashed through the water. Young couples lay under trees, sunbathing. The teeming, excited shouts of kids drifted across from an adventure playground. An aeroplane droned distantly overhead, scoring a white line across the sky. Kerry smelt honeysuckle on the air and the hot sun burnt his face. He liked it here on Saturday afternoon – the relaxed, family outing atmosphere, the shadows of trees playing gently over the grass, the heavy scent of summer all around. He felt good.

"Hey, Trevor!" Tom called. Kerry looked round and saw his older brother standing a few yards away. "Your kid brother here – he's a natural," Tom said.

Trevor glanced nonchalantly at Kerry, then looked at Tom, a derisive smirk on his face. "Come off it, Tom," Trevor said, "you let him take you."

Kerry expected this from Trevor. For some reason, Trevor

usually tried to put him down. "Flaming didn't!" Tom sounded a bit cross with Trevor. "He took the hide off me – didn't you see him?"

"I wasn't watching," Trevor said coolly.

Tom looked at Kerry. "You'll be riding for *The Barons* very shortly, Kerry. Just mark my words."

Kerry grinned with excitement. "Wish I was right now!"

Trevor looked at Kerry and stared at him passively for a brief moment. Then he said: "Know your limits, kid. Stick to the old wall-of-death routine." His voice was flat and dry, monotone, like a radio newsreader's.

"Don't be like that, Trev," said Kerry, "what's the matter with you, hey?"

Trevor looked away. "Fairground stuntsman – that's more your line."

Kerry shrugged. Trevor was often like this, but there was no point in arguing with him. He didn't want a row with his brother. "Well, we'll see, won't we?" was all that he said.

Tom said: "You'll get your chance, Kerry, when the time's right." Tom always stuck up for Kerry when Trevor was in this kind of mood.

"Don't encourage the kid," said Trevor, emphatically.

Kerry spoke quietly, refusing to appear offended by Trevor's remarks. He remained outwardly relaxed. "I don't need encouragement from anyone," he said.

Trevor was silent and continued to watch the racing. Tom glanced anxiously between the two brothers. Kerry grinned and winked at Tom. Then he said to Trevor: "How things going, Trev?"

"Fine." Trevor replied abruptly, keeping his eyes fixed upon the practice track. Kerry sometimes found it hard to believe that he and Trevor were brothers. Their temperaments were completely different, and they didn't even look alike. Trevor was tall and thin, with a lean, rubbery face, and a stern, hawk-like profile. His hair was black and slicked down. He rarely smiled.

Kerry hesitated before he said: "Dad wanted to wish you all the best."

"*Wow*! . . . fantastic!" Trevor remarked, sarcastically. "Made my day, that has."

Kerry squinted at his brother and spoke carefully. "Trev, why don't you come round home sometime and see Dad?"

Trevor didn't want to talk about it. "The old man and me – we've got nothing to say to each other," he said dismissively.

"I reckon he misses you—"

"Then hard luck!" Trevor turned his back on Kerry.

"Come on, Trev!" Kerry persisted. "He's our Dad!"

Trevor looked over his shoulder at Kerry, giving him a hard stare. Trevor spoke quietly, but deliberately: "Listen, kid. I just don't want to know. *Get it*?"

Trevor turned away again. "Tom," he said briskly, "we've got work to do," and began strolling towards a group of riders bent over an upturned motorbike. Tom glanced awkwardly at Kerry, shrugged with a sympathetic smile, then followed Trevor.

Kerry trudged after them, dribbling a lump of coke across the grass. OK, so if that was how Trevor felt, that was the way it would be. He was being as pig-headed as usual, and there was little that Kerry could do about it. One day Trevor and Dad might begin to patch up their differences. And then they could all start behaving like a real family again.

Kerry had caught up with Trevor and Tom. "How did the practice go, Trev?" he asked with a friendly, casual air. "OK?"

" 'Cept for this pot-holed cinder track! What can you do, riding on a base like that?"

Kerry grinned. "Still – come next Sunday afternoon, Trev! Barton Stadium, hey? *Zoom-zoom!*"

"Right-on!" laughed Tom.

Trevor paused, his eyes scanning the practice track. "Big deal!" he snapped. He looked at Kerry, then at Tom. "What are we? *The Barton Barons!*" Trevor's voice was heavy with sarcasm. He said bitterly: "A second division team always matched up against some other tin-pot outfit. It's like playing with plasticine!" Then his eyes wandered across the sports-ground, and beyond to the streets and houses of Barton. His eyes searched restlessly into the distance. He spoke quietly, yet intensely: "I want something better than *this*."

3 Dare-devil

Lacey sat lazily upon his stationary, silent motorbike and looked out along the white, dusty, zig-zagging line of the track, which wound like a long dead snake across the scrubland. His crash helmet hung from one handlebar. He slowly chewed a mouthful of gum as he waited, his eyes fixed on the track in front, watching for signs of an approaching red car. Lacey had been waiting there for nearly half-an-hour. The smooth talker from London was late.

The scrubland stretched from the outskirts of Barton across to the neighbouring town of Weyfield, five miles away. From where Lacey sat, he could just make out the perimeter of Barton through the haze of falling afternoon light, a rim of huddled jerry-built terraces squatting on the near horizon. The scrubland was a dank region of no-man's-land. It was forgotten territory, another world, lying deserted and uninhabited except for the temporary dwelling place of an occasional tramp. Nobody wanted it, nobody cared about it. A bleak, derelict place, pockmarked with gravel craters, black puddles and dead trees. Rubbish dumps stood like scarecrows across the scrubland, tall, silent piles of litter, unwanted tyres, rusted bike frames, skeletons of old cars, broken-down beds, odd bits of discarded furniture. Couch grass, stinging nettles and dry, prickly gorse clung, struggling for life, between the boulders across the dusty ground. The scrubland was not the place for a picnic.

Suddenly the growl of a car engine came from nearby. Lacey

looked up. As if coming from nowhere, like a silent chariot, the red Maxi pulled up fifty yards away from him, the big, circular, cat-like discs of its headlamps watching him. Lacey began walking stiffly towards the vehicle and then paused, waiting, standing in the middle of the track.

"You stay put," Todd told Clayton, "I'll talk to him."

Lacey raised his arm and grinned as Todd approached. "Watchyer, there!" he said, cheerfully.

"Hello, Lacey." Todd's voice was flat, toneless, and he hardly glanced at the youth. He walked past Lacey, left the track, and strolled across the gorse of the scrubland. Lacey followed, glancing nervously at Todd.

"You know something, mister?" asked Lacey. "I can't never remember your name. Daft, ain't it?" he grinned.

Todd paused, and stared at Lacey impassively.

Lacey said: "What *is* it again? *Smith?* . . .*Jones?* Or . . . no, no . . . that's right! *Brown.*"

Lacey chuckled quietly. Todd turned dismissively and continued strolling across the scrubland. Again Lacey followed, dribbling a crushed beer-can along as he walked. He felt out of his depth with Todd, and resented being treated by him like an object, a minion. Best to play along for the moment though, thought Lacey, this bloke's a big-timer, generous with the cash. Keep on the right side of him, and one day *you* could be giving the orders. But he found it difficult to suppress his nervousness.

Finally, Todd spoke. "Tell me how you've been doing, Lacey. How has it gone?"

"Just the way you wanted, Mr Brown. Me and the lads, we've clobbered all the places you said."

"But no one's been hurt?"

Lacey shook his head. "We didn't touch nobody."

"You've kept your visits regular?"

"Like clockwork they're been – every week for the past month."

"And you've been careful to avoid the police?"

Lacey nodded. "Yeah. Soon as we done some place over – off we go, back home to Weyfield."

"And you've kept your activities strictly to the places I instructed you?"

"Right enough." Lacey grinned. "They've all had a touch of knuckle!"

Todd stopped. He said quietly: "How about *The King Cinder?*"

"Oh yes, Mr Brown," Lacey said eagerly, "we've done our extra special treatment there. Business definitely not as usual at *The King Cinder.* Just like you wanted . . ."

Todd was staring into the distance at the black birds circling in the sky. "You've done well, Lacey," he said. "I'm pleased."

Lacey grinned enthusiastically and watched Todd take a thick, bulging, unsealed envelope from his inside jacket pocket. "There are one hundred pounds in here, as you were promised," Todd told him. "Share it out."

"Thanks!"

But Todd didn't hand the envelope to Lacey. He watched the youth for a moment and then waved the envelope in Lacey's face. Then he spoke deliberately: "But there's one very important condition, Lacey. Your work is now finished. No more visits. No more harassment."

Lacey could hardly believe his ears. He stared dumbfounded. "*What?*"

"You're to cause no more trouble in Barton," Todd added.

Lacey swallowed. "You – you're paying us off?"

"You done all that's required of you."

"I thought we'd only just got started!"

Todd shook his head slowly and firmly. "No. No more."

Lacy still couldn't believe it. "Just like *that?*"

"Just like that," Todd said.

Lacey ran his tongue over his lips. "I don't get this!"

"It's simple. I want you and your mates to keep well clear of Barton." Todd paused. "Understood?"

Todd held out the envelope, but Lacey swung angrily away He stared down into a large gravel pit which lay beside them. "You came down from the city a month back. Found me. Found the lads. Chatted us up, got our number." He suddenly looked round at Todd, his face hard and rigid. As Todd did not reply, Lacey's voice thickened with mounting anger. "Found out who we were, what we were about. Everything! *I want you and your mates to ride in on Barton,* you said. *Create a little havoc. Smash a few places up.* You made promises!"

"We made a straightforward deal, pure and simple," Todd said quietly.

"A right screwy deal!" spat Lacey. "Not so pure, not so simple! You *used* us!"

"Lacey, don't waste my time. Take your money and go home."

Then Lacey shouted: "Oh *no*! You picked the wrong sucker here! I'm not playing pawn . . ."

Lacey paced slowly up to Todd and then began walking round him in a circle, holding himself in a stealthy, cat-like, menacing poise. "Who are you, *Mister Brown*?"

Todd yawned. "Go home, Lacey," he said.

Lacey jabbed a finger at Todd's face. "What's your racket, hey? You've been dead worried about us steering clear of coppers. What's going on down here? What's happening in Barton?"

Todd looked away from Lacey, across the scrubland. "Nothing that concerns you."

All right, thought Lacey, *have a go!* Screw all you can out of this beggar, what have you got to lose? "Certain people might be very interested," he said.

Todd looked quickly back at Lacey. "That would bring you a lot of trouble, Lacey!"

Got him! thought Lacey. Right, mister, now you're going to sweat! "An anonymous phone call is cheap and easy," smiled Lacey. "*Nine-nine-nine* and no names . . ."

Todd waved the envelope. "It'll lose you *this*."

Lacey breathed tensely. He had the smoothie on the run, but his nerves were jangling. "It's going to cost you *two* hundred to stop that phone call," Lacey said. "Just for starters."

Todd laughed suddenly. It was the laugh of a man whose mind was not laughing. "Lacey," he said patiently, "you're way out of your depth. You don't know what you're mixing in. Find some sense."

Take the devil by the horns, thought Lacey, show him what you're made of! "Well, Mr Brown, the way things stand, I reckon I got you over a barrel. So I want *in* with your scheme." Lacey smiled. He was feeling more confident now. He was going to get his own way. "Or the police get my phone call."

Both men stood there in silence for a moment, staring at each other. There was a swift, sharp movement from Todd as he gave Lacey a short, sharp punch in the stomach. Lacey grunted heavily, doubling up as he held his stomach, sobbing with pain.

Todd remained calm, looking down at the bent figure. "Lacey, I've dealt with hundreds of back-street yobs like you. You're all the same. Useful while you last, but when the time comes to wave bye-bye, the whining starts."

Clayton climbed quickly out of the car and began walking towards Todd and Lacey. Todd waved at him, indicating that he should stay where he was. Clayton leaned against the car bonnet and watched.

Lacey eased himself up slowly, massaging his stomach. He looked at Todd. "*You*—"

Suddenly Todd grabbed Lacey by his hair and violently pulled his head back. Lacey winced with pain.

"How do you make out with the birds, Lacey?" Todd asked. "Fancy you, don't they? Down at the disco of a Saturday night? A handsome lad like you. Make out all right, don't you?"

"I—"

Todd released Lacey, then suddenly pushed him backwards. Lacey yelled as he tumbled head-first into the pit, sending up an explosion of tiny stones as he fell.

Todd stepped to the edge of the pit and stood there, legs astride, as he looked down at Lacey sprawled out below. Lacey began coughing violently, twisted over, and began wiping the dust from his face and eyes.

Todd lit a small cigar. "Keep thinking of those clean-cut looks, Lacey. Because if there's any trouble from you, any trouble from your mates, then *I* make a phone call . . ."

Lacey stared dumbly up at Todd. Todd was holding his cigar between the fingers of one hand, looking at the lighted tip. "A phone call to a professional. He'll come looking for you." Todd smiled. "And he won't be nice."

Lacey's voice was thin and scared. "There'll be no trouble," he said, "I promise it!"

There was a pause as Todd regarded Lacey. "Right," said Todd, and he tossed the unsealed envelope up into the air. The pound notes fell out and, caught in the breeze, fluttered down like leaves on top of Lacey until the money lay scattered around him. Todd pointed with his cigar. "If *you* or any of your mates show up in Barton . . . then I wouldn't like to be you, Lacey, waking up of a morning, looking at your face in the mirror."

Panic had gripped Lacey and he stammered badly. "Anything you s-say . . ."

"Keep life simple," Todd advised.

"Yes, Mr B-Brown . . ."

Todd then walked briskly back towards the car.

Clayton was still waiting by the vehicle. "Everything OK?" he asked.

"Oh, yes," Todd replied coolly as he climbed into the car.

Lacey brushed the dust off his clothes and began quickly gathering up the pound notes scattered around him. He glanced round to watch as the red car cruised away down the track towards Barton, leaving a screen of dust along the twisting path.

Todd stared blankly out through the windscreen as he steered carefully round the bends of the narrow track.

"What now?" asked Clayton.

Todd tossed his cigar butt out of the open window. "Now the King," he said.

Nikki sat among the crowds in the wall-of-death marquee and watched Kerry enter the base of the pit, riding the fairground's big, shining red dare-devil motorbike. Kerry raised one hand to the crowd. Some of the spectators clapped and there were a few cheers. Then Kerry revved up the motorbike and began circling the pit, gradually increasing speed, until the roar of the engine was deafening. The bike moved gradually outwards, in ever increasing circles, so that finally Kerry reached the outer perimeter of the pit and circled the base of the wall itself. The wall-of-death was a tall, circular, self-enclosed, vertical prism. Kerry hunched himself over the motorbike, throwing his weight on to one side, easing the machine over so that it moved forward poised sideways at an extreme angle. Nikki looked quickly away as Kerry thrust the bike upwards, pitching it up on to the wall.

Nikki felt her heart flutter. She sat listening, her eyes shut tight, waiting for the crash to come. But there was no crash. There never was. Nikki had seen Kerry ride the wall-of-death dozens of times but, however much Kerry had tried to reassure her, Nikki was always afraid something would go wrong. She opened her eyes and looked back down into the pit. Kerry was now circling the bottom of the wall, riding the motorbike horizontally around the interior of the prism. The crowd had begun clapping and cheering, a few teenage girls whistling shrilly with excitement. Nikki resented the spectators that came here, chewing their hot-dogs and striped sticks of rock, paying hard cash in the hope of seeing some stunt rider fetch it. That was what it was all about! A few cheap thrills, with Kerry down there risking his neck. Kerry claimed that dare-devil riding looked more dangerous than it actually was, he said he rode at a much slower speed than appeared, and it was all a bit of a con-trick. Nikki didn't believe him. One day there would be an accident and she would be proved right.

Now Kerry began gradually climbing the side of the prism, up towards the top, where the spectators sat on benches round the outside of the wall, or stood at the mouth of the prism, looking in. Many of the spectators were clustered around the top of the wall, peering down as Kerry rode up towards them, crawling the side of the prism like a fly in a jam-jar. Nikki eyed the crowd coldly as they watched Kerry career round and round the wall below. She was sitting on a bench near the front of the auditorium.

Kerry was now two-thirds the way up the wall, circling it swiftly. Suddenly he let go of the handlebars and held up his arms in a big, showmanlike gesture, riding now without hands. This was all part of the ritual. The crowd began clapping and cheering enthusiastically. Nikki just sat there longing for the stunt to end. This was Kerry's final performance that evening.

Kerry gripped the handlebars again and then moved the bike in a pattern across the side of the wall, skilfully describing an arc with the movement of the machine. This brought more clapping from the spectators. Then Kerry thrust the motorbike upwards, towards the top of the wall, finally reaching its upper rim, very close to the crowd. The spectators standing behind the barricade stepped quickly back as the red bike flashed up like a shark just below them and spun swiftly round the very top of the prism. A few people looked a bit scared, some of the girls in the crowd clung on to their boyfriends. Nikki smiled wryly to herself.

Kerry had climbed the wall-of-death and now zoomed loudly round the top of it, the clapping and cheering of the crowd completely drowned by the intense roar of the engine. Kerry suddenly let go of the handlebars, once again riding without hands, holding out his arms expansively. The crowd cheered and whistled. They were certainly getting their money's worth tonight.

Kerry took hold of the handlebars and then gradually, gracefully, wound the motorbike downwards, spiralling down, down, across the wall, until he was circling the bottom of the prism, then carefully manoeuvred the bike back on to the base of the pit. Nikki let out a sigh of relief. Kerry rode the bike to the centre, then dismounted and took a bow. The crowd cheered. Some of the spectators began tossing coins down into the pit. Nikki pursed her lips and gathered up her handbag. Kerry bowed again as more coins landed on the floor around him. Nikki stood up from the bench and walked stiffly towards the exit. Her face and hands were sweaty, and her T-shirt stuck to her back.

Nikki left the marquee and went round to the back where Kerry's motorbike was parked. At least the fairground provided their own bike for the wall-of-death stunt, which meant that it was carefully checked over for safety before each performance. Nikki sat on the grass beside Kerry's bike. She never quite understood why she came each week to watch Kerry. But it was preferable to sitting at home worrying.

Kerry, carrying his leather jacket over one arm, emerged from the marquee and came over to Nikki, grinning, holding out two handfuls of loose change for her to see. "That's not bad, is it?" He stuffed the coins into his pockets.

Nikki stood up and strolled casually across to him. "Buy me some candyfloss, then," she said.

Kerry and Nikki strolled across the fairground, each licking huge explosions of candyfloss. The fair was packed with milling Saturday night crowds. The air was hot and greasy and music bubbled from the side-shows. The big wheel, illuminated by red and yellow lights, turned slowly, looming majestically over the fairground. Kids laughed and shrieked with excitement on the dodgem rink. Neon lights winked brightly from the merry-go-round and a bingo contest was being announced over a loud-speaker. A boxing side-show had attracted a small crowd. Its promoter stood on a platform next to a boxer adorned in a shining silver cape, who slapped grimly at a punch-ball.

Kerry loved the fair. Dad often talked about the old Barton fair, what it used to be like years back, when there were freak shows and talking horses, genuine gypsy fortune-tellers and man-eating tigers. Now it had been cleaned up and modernised. But that didn't matter to Kerry. It was just good to be there, to be out on a Saturday night, among so many people enjoying themselves.

Kerry glanced at Nikki. She had been a bit moody tonight, not much to say for herself. "Coming to the speedway next Sunday, then?" Kerry asked her brightly.

"Don't I always?" said Nikki, in a matter-of-fact tone. She was obviously down-in-the-dumps over something.

Kerry grinned. "Yeah! Bubbling with enthusiasm and all! A real A-one fan!"

Nikki shrugged casually. "Just gets a bit boring," was all she said.

"Got no soul, have you?"

Nikki gave him a wry look. "Going to give me the elbow, then? Find a proper speedway freak to knock around with?"

Kerry pretended to take the suggestion seriously. "Let you know when I've thought about it."

"Have to rest up first," advised Nikki.

"Eh . . .?"

"Thinking – it can tire you!"

Kerry grinned. "How would you know?" he asked.

Nikki turned suddenly and planted her sponge of candyfloss right in the middle of Kerry's face. "Take that!" she said, laughing, pushing the candyfloss right up Kerry's nose.

Kerry pulled away. "Hey, get off!" Kerry tried to wipe the sticky floss from his face.

"Serves you right," giggled Nikki.

Kerry licked his lips. "You know what? Your candyfloss tastes better than mine!"

"Well," said Nikki, "I *deserve* better."

"On a good day!" grinned Kerry. Nikki seemed more herself now, but Kerry still wondered what was bothering her.

They walked on past a ten-pin bowling alley. Then Nikki said: "Kerry . . . you serious about taking up speedway racing?" Her tone was more anxious.

Kerry glanced at Nikki, frowning. "Yeah, course I am!"

"What for? Risking your neck."

So *that* was it! First Dad, now Nikki. But Kerry didn't feel in the mood for an argument tonight, so he just shrugged it off. "Well, it's *my* neck!" he joked.

"Just a great big ego trip, isn't it?" said Nikki, trying to provoke him.

"I've heard that record before."

Nikki persisted. "Look at me! Here I am! Kerry Hutson! Champion of the world!"

"Go and jump in the lake," said Kerry with a laugh.

Nikki pulled a face at him, cross at his nonchalance. Kerry blew a kiss at her and grinned. Nikki turned away. "Tarzan on a big red scooter!" she scoffed.

4 Todd

Richard Hutson yawned. It had been a long day. Saturdays were always busy during the holiday season. And then there had been that trouble with those Weyfield yobs this morning . . . he must remember to look into that business tomorrow, yes, have a word with some of his mates down at the local. He rung open the till and began removing cash from the drawer.

He heard footsteps smacking along the pavement outside and saw two silhouetted figures moved behind the venetian blinds. Passers-by . . .

He begun counting the day's taking. A sudden, heavy banging on the restaurant door pierced the silence, and he dropped a handful of coins in surprise. Who on *earth* . . .?

Through the drifting shadows he saw the two silhouetted figures framed behind the restaurant door. Burglars? Then the knocking came again, rattling the door. Must be trouble of some sort, burglars would hardly announce their presence. Unless they hoped to take him by surprise . . .

Then came a hoarse, insistent voice: "Police! Urgent! Open up at once!"

He stiffened. *Police* . . . something's happened to Kerry . . . an accident at the fairground . . .

"All right!" he called as he weaved his way between chairs and tables across the darkened interior. "I'm coming . . ."

He unbolted the door, which immediately swung back in his face, knocking him violently into the restaurant. He went crashing into the tables and chairs as he tumbled to the floor.

He scrambled quickly to his feet. "*What!*"

Todd and Clayton barged in. Clayton pointed the automatic at him. "Stay where you are, Hutson," he said.

Todd closed the door and bolted it securely. "Hello, Hutson," he said quietly.

Richard Hutson stared at the tall, sturdy figure. "Who . . ." But no, he'd never forget that voice, even though it sounded more refined now, more sophisticated. He recognised the man's frame, the way he held himself. Despite the darkness, he could make out the familiar hardness of his jaw.

"*Todd* . . ." his voice rasped . . . "Todd Edwards! What the hell are *you* doing here?"

"There are certain things we have to talk about," Todd said.

"Talk . . .?"

"Some matters of mutual interest." Todd gestured across the interior. "But first let us find somewhere more private, yes?"

Richard Hutson stepped forward and shouted angrily: "Get out right now!"

Clayton raised the automatic and pointed it at his forehead.

"I don't think so," smiled Todd.

Richard Hutson entered the living-room, crossed over and turned on the main light. Clayton followed closely, still covering him with the automatic. Todd stepped inside, closed the door, and glanced round the room.

"Yes, very nice too . . ." Todd noticed a bookcase in the corner. Its shelves were lined with cups and shields which had been won at speedway tournaments. Todd smiled to himself.

"What do you want?" Richard Hutson asked firmly.

Todd ignored the question. "Your son – Kerry. Where is he?"

"Out. He'll be back later on."

"So we're alone in the house?"

"Yes."

"Good." Todd smiled blandly. He glanced at Clayton, who still held the automatic. "I don't think we'll be needing that any more, providing the King here behaves himself."

Clayton slid the weapon into his jacket pocket. He leant up against a wall, keeping his eyes on Hutson.

Todd lit a cigar. "Right, down to business. I've come to make you an offer, Hutson."

He eyed Todd suspiciously. "What kind of offer?"

"An offer of protection," began Todd. "I believe that you are in need of it."

"Really?"

"You've been having some trouble lately. With motorbike gangs. Arriving here and causing trouble in your restaurant."

"So you're behind it!"

"I understand other people in Barton have had similar trouble." Todd shook his head sadly, then smiled. "Tut-tut! These vandals! But it's true, isn't it? Barton has seen quieter times?"

"So it's you!"

"But *I'm* here to protect you. I also want to protect your fellow businessmen."

Todd crossed to the sideboard and poured himself a drink. "You're a powerful man in this town, with a great deal of influence. People listen to you. You could be mayor of Barton if you chose."

"*And?*"

"And now I want it like this," said Todd. "I will provide protection against this very reprehensible vandalism." Todd topped up his scotch with soda water. He turned and looked at Hutson. "But it has to be paid for. By you. And by your fellow proprietors here in Barton."

"I see . . ." said Hutson, quietly.

Todd sipped his drink. "So I want you to let it be known that you have agreed to my arrangements. And to see to it that everyone else does the same. Understood?"

Clayton was listening intently. His eyes flipped back and forth between the two men. At last he was learning something of Todd's scheme.

"And how much will this *protection* service cost us?"

"One hundred pounds a week from each of you."

Hutson gave a hard, sarcastic laugh. "You're crazy!"

"Take it seriously, Hutson," Todd warned. "Or you'll have bother."

"You think a few yobs on motorbikes worry me? You think they can't be handled?"

Todd flicked ash on to the carpet. "What you've had so far, that's just the start," he said.

Hutson strode across the room, towards Todd. "Just why have you come back here to Barton?"

"It's simple," smiled Todd. "I decided to pay a visit to my home town. I didn't want Barton to forget me."

"You were always the trouble-maker in this town! Vandalism, petty crime, terrorising kids – you name it!"

"I never claimed to be a model citizen," Todd said, blandly.

"Well, Barton didn't reckon much on you. We taught you a lesson or two!"

"I remember."

"Pity some of it didn't stick."

Todd spoke softly, with a cold intensity: "Oh, it stuck right enough. Not the way it was intended to, perhaps. But it's all there, Hutson, stored in my memory."

"You got what was coming to you."

Todd stared, his eyes pinned on to Hutson's face. "Oh no, you made it personal. Turned it into a vendetta. You *hounded* me!"

Hutson was momentarily stunned by Todd's sudden vehemence. "I dealt out what was coming, cut you down to size and sent you packing," he said, adding sarcastically: "The last I heard you'd gone off to the big city to make your fortune."

"That's right." Todd swallowed the remainder of his drink. "And I've done that."

"I wonder how!"

Todd smiled, and placed his empty glass on the sideboard. He strolled over to the bookcase and lifted one of the prize cups, inspecting it closely. "Yes, you're right," he said. "Getting to the top can present its problems. You have to use the old elbow a bit, don't you, Hutson? You need to put the boot in now and again if you want to get to the top like you did." Todd replaced the cup. "To win that all important crown, hey? Yes, there are one or two skeletons in your cupboard, aren't there, King?"

Hutson stared at Todd. He was speechless.

Todd sat down in an armchair. "I happen to know that you haven't always played it clean and straight. The legend and the truth – they don't quite tally."

There was a long silence. Hutson turned slowly away, bent forward as if suddenly struck by sickness. He placed his back to Todd and Clayton. When he spoke, his voice was dry and crisp, like the sound of a biscuit breaking: "International sport . . . it – it can be a dirty business."

"And you weren't averse to playing it dirty on occasions, were you?"

"Sometimes . . . often . . . it's a case of dog eat dog . . ." Hutson's voice was almost a whisper now, as if he was speaking to himself.

"Quite," Todd smiled. "And everyone has their price."

Clayton, standing by the wall, was grinning broadly. He was enjoying every moment.

Hutson turned and spoke anxiously to Todd: "All right, maybe I didn't always go strictly by the book—"

Todd laughed. "Quite an understatement, *that*, Hutson!"

"Look, all this is ancient history now. Who's going to trouble themselves over what happened years back?"

"*This* town will trouble over it. This town where you're King. Where that means something."

"And who do you think's going to believe *you*?"

Todd stared steadily at Hutson. "I'm sure the local newspapers will, if I tell it right. And I will. Then Barton will turn very mean. Everything you've got here – your reputation, your business, your whole way of life . . . this town will destroy it."

"And of course," Todd added, when Hutson made no comment, "your sons who admire you so much, they will be the first to know . . ."

Todd stood up slowly and tossed his cigar butt into the grate. He had decided that it was time to leave. Hutson would come round, eventually. He didn't really have much choice. Todd walked to the door. "You'll be hearing from me, Hutson."

"Look! It's a crazy idea! How can I persuade other people

in this town to pay protection money to *you*? To Todd Edwards of all people! How can I?"

Todd shrugged. "It's your problem."

"I can't do it!" shouted Hutson.

Todd studied his face for a moment. "Unless you get this town to co-operate, I'll ruin you here in Barton. With what I know." Todd wagged a finger at him. "*Facts.* Dates and places. Money that changed hands. The names of all the people who got trodden on so that *you* could get to the top."

Hutson suddenly waved an arm in dismissal. "No!" he said, bluntly. "I won't do it! Now get out of my house!" He pointed angrily at Clayton. "And take your bulldog with you!"

"Right." Todd opened the door. "You're finished, Hutson," he promised. "Finished for good . . . ."

Kerry had taken Nikki home, and now he roared down the High Street, swung past the restaurant, and drew up at the mouth of the back lane. He leant his bike against the granite wall, and was unstrapping his helmet when he heard the door of the restaurant open and footsteps echo along the pavement. Kerry frowned. The restaurant had been closed a couple of hours.

"Hey, Todd . . ." Kerry heard the voice, glanced round, and saw the two men crossing the street. "So what happens next . . ." The one who spoke was short and fat, but Kerry couldn't make out either men clearly through the darkness. They walked off, out of ear-shot.

Kerry shrugged. Probably business acquaintances of his father's. He watched the two men cross over to a car parked in the side-street opposite, and climb in. The headlights burst on, their beams reflected across the chassis of the vehicle. Kerry could see that the car was a blood-red Maxi. It moved forward and swung into the high street.

Kerry walked up the lane towards the back of the house, leaving his bike against the wall. He was feeling tired, it was late, so he would put the bike away in the garage next morning.

The kitchen was in darkness, but a shaft of light splashed

through from the living-room. Kerry heard a movement and looked in. He saw his father standing by the bookcase, staring down at the cups and shields. He was in his shirt sleeves, and looked sweaty and dishevelled. Kerry opened his mouth to speak, but the words died in his mouth as he saw his father suddenly grasp one of the prize-cups in both hands, and throw it with all his might at the far wall. The cup crashed loudly and tumbled to the floor.

Kerry gasped. "*Dad!*"

His father looked round. His face was sweating. He stared woodenly at Kerry, as if not seeing him at all. Then he looked slowly away, wiping his hand wearily across his face.

Kerry stepped inside the living-room. "What's happened?" His father was silent, standing in the same position, as if a mixer-load of cement had been poured over him. Kerry stole up to him. "Is there some trouble?"

His father shook his head slowly. "No," he said, quietly. "No trouble . . ."

Kerry nodded at the dented prize-cup lying on the floor. "What you blow your top for just then?" he asked.

His father wouldn't look him straight in the eye. "Nothing that concerns you," he said abruptly.

Kerry stared at him. Something was badly wrong, he'd never seen him behave this way before. "Who were those two blokes?"

His father looked round quickly. "What?" he asked sharply.

"The two blokes that came out of the restaurant just now, drove off in a red car."

"Customers," said his father dismissively. "Just customers . . ."

Kerry could tell that he was lying. "Bit late, weren't they? Restaurant's been closed a couple of hours."

"Slow eaters. Took their time." His father moved restlessly over to the table, and began gathering up some crockery.

Kerry remained unconvinced. "Who were they, Dad?" he pressed.

"I told you! Customers!"

Kerry stiffened. His father sometimes lost his temper like everyone else, but this time it was something much more. He wasn't just angry – he was frightened about something. Kerry came up to him and spoke quietly: "Who were they, Dad? What did they want?"

He moved away from Kerry, avoiding his steady gaze. "Go to bed, Kerry."

"Why won't you tell me?"

Then he slapped the table surface with the flat of his hand. "Look!" he shouted angrily. "Do as you're told and get to bed!" And turned his back on Kerry.

Kerry could see that his father was shaking slightly, and he felt completely out of his depth. He opened the door and quietly left the room.

Kerry stayed awake all night, lying on top of his bed, fully dressed. He heard his father moving about once or twice downstairs. But he didn't come up to bed. Finally, the stillness of the small, dead hours descended upon the household. Kerry lay there, listening to the night.

His father had acted completely out of character, smashing that speedway cup against the wall! Dad would never do such a thing normally, no matter how angry he got. He took huge pride in those prize-cups, polishing them regularly every Sunday. Perhaps that was it . . . something to do with speedway . . . but dad's speedway days were over and done with . . . or could it be connected with Trevor in some way? But that couldn't be it, they hadn't seen each other for months.

Those men who left the restaurant just as Kerry arrived . . . they were definitely something to do with it. Dad had become cagey and really het-up when Kerry asked who they were. He tried to recall the snippet of conversation he had heard between the two strangers. One of them, the small fat man, had called the other by his name. Kerry struggled to remember. Todd . . . yes . . . that was it. *Todd.* But Todd *who?*

The hazy strands of first light weaved in through the gap in the curtains and filled out across the room. Pigeons were calling on the roof outside, their feet scratching on the tiles. Kerry climbed off the bed, drew back the curtains, and peered outside. Row upon row of terraced houses sat shrouded and silent.

High-rise blocks of flats silhouetted against the rising light looked like tall ghosts. A long-distance lorry moaned past nearby, echoing down the vacant streets. Kerry glanced at his watch. It was nearly six o'clock.

He stole out of his bedroom and stood on the landing, listening intently. The house was silent. He crept down to the kitchen and peered tentatively through the living-room door. His father was lying stretched out on the settee, asleep. Kerry watched him for a moment. The speedway cup still lay on the floor. Suddenly, Kerry felt a powerful urge to go, to leave the house. He moved stealthily to the back door.

Outside the air was crisp and cool. Kerry breathed in deep lungfulls, like a drowning man. A church clock struck six, a distant, tinny sound which melted into the sleeping stillness. Kerry crept down the back lane where he had left his motorbike. He heard a milk float move off down the street, the rattle of milk bottles in crates, the stop-start purr of the engine. He strapped on his helmet, pushed the bike to the mouth of the lane and mounted it.

Maybe it should be left well alone, thought Kerry, as he rode down the empty streets. Perhaps he shouldn't poke his nose in. After all, his father was perfectly capable of managing his own affairs. And he wouldn't thank Kerry for interfering. But Kerry just couldn't remain indifferent to something like this. Dad was in some kind of trouble, perhaps bad trouble. And that involved Kerry whether he liked it or not. Maybe he wouldn't be able to help. But at least he could try.

It was strange seeing the town at this time of the morning. All the familiar places looked different, and the deserted street corners took on an odd appearance. Kerry felt guilty as he rode along the still rows. He tried to keep the motorbike engine as quiet as possible, imagining that at any moment all the doors of the houses would burst open and people would stand there, angrily waving their fists at him for disturbing their Sunday morning lie-in. He was relieved when at last he swung into the coastal road.

Kerry knew that old Nulty would be up and around early this morning, down on the shore, beach-combing, gathering up the leftovers from the Saturday crowds. Nulty was like a grandfather to him. He lived in an old boat-house where he and Kerry would spend many an hour drinking home-made cider and playing cards. He would tell and, at Kerry's insistence, often retell, stories of his past speedway exploits. Kerry would sit there, on the boat-verandah, enchanted by the old man's memories, no matter how many times he had heard them before.

Many years ago, Nulty had ridden for *The Barons*. He was all set for a career as a professional, but at one meeting his bike crashed and Nulty barely survived the accident. He remained crippled in one leg, and still walked with a bad limp. Nulty never rode the track again. He bought the boat-house with what savings he had, and opened up a fish-stall in the town, managing to scrape a living. He seemed contented enough these days but he really looked forward to Kerry's visits, and didn't at all mind recalling his past life on the track.

But Kerry had a special reason for visiting Nulty that morning. Nulty was the one person in the whole of Barton who really knew his father. They had grown up together and attended the same school. They both rode for *The Barons*. His father had been made captain of the team just a few months before the accident, and had been very good to Nulty, getting him special hospital treatment, lending him money and helping him adjust to his new way of life. If anyone could help Kerry find out what was bugging dad, then it was Nulty.

The coastal road was deserted except for a few fishermen stoically guarding their rods. The tide was out and the disc of the blue-grey sea sat sedately in the distance. Seagulls heckled overhead. Kerry left the road, bouncing his bike across the pavement, the machine tearing through the undergrowth of wild heather along the sandy path which led to the beach. Kerry skidded down the twisting track and rode out to the shingle, then paused, squinting along the shore. Yes, sure enough, there was Nulty, pushing an old battered pram, supporting himself with a thick, heavy-looking walking stick. Kerry revved up the motorbike engine and rode slowly, in a zig-zag pattern, across the shifting sand, out towards Nulty.

Nulty wore a string vest and a pair of old baggy trousers held up by a length of rope. His pram was piled high with odds and ends he had been busily gathering up from the beach. He heard the roar of the motorbike and turned, smiling broadly as he saw Kerry approach.

"Wotchyer there, Nulty!" Kerry called as he drew up beside the pram. Kerry dismounted, lowered his bike so that it rested on the soft sand, and unstrapped his helmet. "Thought I'd find you down here first thing on Sunday morning!" he grinned. "How y'doing, then? All right?"

Nulty was a Liverpool-Irishman and spoke in a gruff, thick accent. "Aye, aye!" he bellowed deeply.

Kerry peered into the pram. "What've you found?" he asked. "Anything good?" There were several pairs of sandals, a neat pile of sunglasses, and a plastic box containing some dried, curled-up sandwiches. A couple of unopened tins of Coke, some packets of crisps, plenty of plastic knives, forks and spoons. There were a number of towels and T-shirts as well. But the prize find was a smart brown-and-red transistor radio. Kerry held it up. "Hey, that's not bad! Someone will have to do without Tony Blackburn for a bit!" Kerry took hold of the pram, and pushed it along. "Come on, give you a hand."

"Ta, lad." Nulty limped along beside Kerry, scanning the beach for more finds.

After a moment, Kerry glanced at Nulty and then spoke awkwardly, a little diffidently. "Came down here for a reason this morning," he explained. "Had to talk to you."

"Aye?"

"It's about Dad," Kerry said.

Nulty sensed something was wrong. "Dick all right, is he?"

Then Kerry spotted something lying on the sand. "Hey!" he exclaimed, suddenly. "A pair of plimsolls!" He bounced over and picked up a pair of grubby-looking plimsolls, sniffed them, pulled a face, and plonked them in the pram. "Sweaty feet . . ." he grimaced.

Kerry pushed the pram on across the sand, Nulty trudging beside him. "Thing is, Nulty, you and Dad rode together for

The Barons." Kerry looked at Nulty. "So you know him, *really* know him."

"Aye," said Nulty, "maybe . . ."

There was a pause. Then Kerry said: "Well, I reckon he's in some sort of trouble."

Nulty looked round. "Trouble?"

"Late last night, when I got home, he was in a bad way."

"What about, lad?"

Kerry shook his head. "Wouldn't let on, hardly said a word. There were these two blokes that left just as I got home. They drove a red Maxi car. Know the sort of job I mean?" Nulty nodded. "Those two blokes, I reckon they put Dad on the spot over something."

Nulty frowned. "What they look like?"

"Couldn't see clearly. It was dark, and I wasn't really looking. One of them was short and he had a paunch. Both dressed smart, like they were businessmen."

Kerry picked up a towel strewn across a rock, folded it up neatly, and placed it in the pram. "I overheard them talking as they left. One of them is called Todd."

Nulty suddenly stopped walking and stood there, propped up against his walking stick, staring at Kerry. His face had grown serious. "*Todd?*"

"Yeah," said Kerry. "You know him?"

"Aye lad, that I do," Nulty said quietly. "From way back." He looked away, staring distantly out to sea. "Todd Edwards . . . ."

Ten minutes later Kerry was squatting on the steps of the boat-house verandah, sipping a mug of cider.

"Was Todd a speedway rider?" he asked.

"Naw," spat Nulty. He was unloading the day's catch from the pram, sorting out his finds into neat piles. "Spiv, yobbo. Nasty piece of work was Todd Edwards. Always making trouble in this town, him and his gang of tearaways."

"How did Dad get involved with him?"

"Nobody else would stand up to Todd. Dick put a stop to his tricks." Nulty grinned. "Gave Todd the hiding of his life!"

"What happened?"

"Todd had his belly-full by the time Dick finished with him. So he just shuttled off, left Barton and went to London."

"Maybe that's why he's come back," Kerry said, thoughtfully. "Get his own back on Dad."

Nulty was hanging out the towels and T-shirts along the verandah rail. "Naw!" he said, dismissively. "Not after all this time. Happened years back."

Kerry downed the cider. "It's something serious, Nulty. Dad was in a right state last night, smashed up one of his speedway cups. He hardly ever loses his temper."

"Don't worry y'self, lad," Nulty told him. "Dick'll sort it out!"

Kerry frowned. "I dunno, I'm a bit bothered about it." He hesitated before he said: "Will you talk to Dad, Nulty? See what the trouble is?"

Nulty paused and looked at Kerry. Then he shook his head slowly and spoke to the boy gently: "No, lad. Be no use. He's his own man, wouldn't let me in on it." Nulty scratched his beard. "And, y'know, we're different men now, from the days when we rode together."

Kerry looked disappointed. He shrugged absently. "Yeah, OK . . ."

"Sorry, lad. Just the way it is."

"Best get going," said Kerry, putting the mug down on the table.

"Tell you what," said Nulty, "I'll nose round a bit. Put the word about. Find out what there is to know."

"Thanks, Nulty. I'll see you again soon, OK?" He ran off across the sand, back towards his motorbike. "Cheers then, Nulty!"

5 Hunch

The Barons usually had a Sunday morning practice run on the track at the community sportsground, unless there was a race-meeting at Barton Stadium in the afternoon. Their next meeting wasn't until the following Sunday afternoon, when they were up against *The Weyfield Warriors.*

Kerry parked his motorbike at the side of the practice track and dumped his helmet beside it. He spotted Trevor and Tom standing by the side of the track fifty yards away, both sipping from tins of Coke. They were watching two of their team riders battle it out on the practice track. Kerry normally turned up to most of the sessions, but today he had a particular reason for doing so. He wanted to find out what Trevor knew about Todd Edwards, if anything.

Kerry called across as he approached: "Trev! Tom! Wotchyer, there!"

Trevor glanced briefly at his younger brother, then looked back at the racing. He said nothing. Tom grinned broadly at Kerry. "Kerry! All right, then?" He picked out a tin of Coke from a cardboard box on the ground, and tossed it to Kerry.

Kerry caught the tin. "Ta!" He took a long swig. "How's it going?" he asked Tom.

Tom grinned. "Come next Sunday afternoon, we're going to tear Weyfield apart! They won't know what hit them!"

Trevor spoke for the first time. "Toppling Weyfield is chicken feed!" he sneered. "We wouldn't be matched against second division teams if it weren't for our crumb-bum of a captain over there . . ."

Trevor nodded along the side of the track towards a blonde-haired, anaemic-looking man in his late thirties, who was talking to some of the riders as he sipped coffee from a plastic cup. His name was Campbell, the current captain of *The Barons*.

"Well, he's past it right enough," said Tom, looking at Campbell. "And he knows it."

As they talked, the Maxi nosed slowly up the tarmac road and pulled to a halt near the practice track. Todd and Clayton climbed out.

Trevor still eyed his team-captain malevolently. "He won't budge though, will he?" Trevor said bitterly. "Clinging on like a limpet!"

Tom told him: "Everyone knows you'll get made captain, Trevor, one day soon."

"Not soon enough!" said Trevor intensely. "I want to take *The Barons* into the first division. And *fast!*"

Tom grinned. "Patience, lad!" he said, and turned his attention back to the track.

"Trev," said Kerry, "did you ever hear of a guy called Todd?"

Trevor frowned. "Todd?" he asked. "Todd who?"

"Todd Edwards."

"Never heard of him."

"Dad never talked about him, mentioned him at all?"

Trevor shook his head. "Not that I remember. Why?"

Kerry shrugged it off. "Don't matter," he said casually.

Tom squinted across the sportsground as his eye caught something. The sunlight made Todd's field glasses glint brightly and the two lenses shone like cats' eyes. "Hey, look!" said Tom. "We're being watched. Over there – that bloke with the binoculars."

Kerry followed Tom's gaze. He stiffened as he saw the red Maxi and the two smartly-dressed men standing beside it. So they were here. The short fat one. And the tall, sturdy one watching through field glasses . . . Todd.

"Do you know who they are?" Kerry asked quietly.

Trevor glanced at him. "What?"

"Those men. Who are they?"

"Trippers most likely," suggested Tom.

Kerry saw Todd and the fat man climb back into the car which then slid smoothly away. Kerry made an instant decision. He wasn't going to lose them now!

Kerry turned quickly and plonked his tin of Coke into Tom's hands, so that suddenly Tom found himself forced to grip hold of the extra tin. He looked round, startled. "Kerry, *what—*"

But Kerry had gone, racing across the cropped grass towards his motorbike. He grabbed his helmet, pushed it on to his head, fastening the strap as he released the parking-stand and mounted the bike. He kicked the machine into action, revving the engine into an ugly growl. He ripped across the grassy slopes and the bike bounced heavily on to the road and tore along it. Through his visor, Kerry saw the car turn off and enter the town's one-way system. Kerry hunched himself over his machine and ground swiftly along.

The car circled a roundabout and bore left down a dual-carriageway. Kerry followed behind at a discreet distance, camouflaging himself among the steady stream of holiday traffic, yet keeping the vehicle clearly in his sights. The route Todd had adopted showed that he knew the town well. They were travelling towards the country.

Gradually, the traffic thinned and Kerry graded his speed accordingly, maintaining a healthy stretch of road between himself and the red car. Church bells pealed out across the surrounding fields and meadows. Members of a congregation piled out of a small country church at the close of morning service.

Kerry followed his quarry through thick woodlands. Here the road narrowed considerably and families of picnickers occupied its grassy verges. The Maxi swung left and forked off down a narrow lane. Kerry knew immediately where Todd was heading.

He decided on a short cut, turned the bike off the side of

the road and plunged through the ferns into the woods. Negotiating his way skilfully through the trees, Kerry bore down towards a woodland path which led to a vantage point overlooking the woods. Here Kerry paused, looking down over the tree-tops towards the narrow lane. The red car flashed along it under the branches. Yes, Todd was heading for the canal.

Kerry cruised downhill and rode along the mossy bank of a river, past a clutch of tents where some boy scouts had made camp. He forked off and came out at a clearing overlooking the canal. Here the country lane had given way to a wide gravel track beside the canal. Three barges, spaced about a hundred yards apart, were moored along the quiet stretch of water. Kerry heard a car approach. He dismounted, propped the bike against the trunk of an old oak tree, removed his helmet and hid it among the ferns, then crouched in the undergrowth to watch.

The Maxi nosed along the gravel track and came into view, pulling up beside the third barge, which lay at the most isolated point along the canal. Kerry crawled through the undergrowth and found himself a hiding place overlooking the barge.

Todd and his companion climbed out of the car. Their shoes crunched on the gravel track as they walked towards the barge.

"What time is this bloke due to arrive?" asked the fat one.

"At twelve," Todd replied crisply.

Kerry glanced at his watch. It was quarter-to. *What bloke?* Kerry wondered. He would soon find out. He watched the two men clamber on to the barge. Todd unlocked the cabin door and they went inside.

Kerry waited impatiently. He could see both men sitting inside the cabin. A gentle breeze moved across the flat, motionless water, rustling the thick reeds embedded along its banks. Bright sunlight slanted mysteriously through the woods in a hot, seductive mist. Leaves were reflected in playful patterns across the red stones of the gravel track. Some fishermen sat eating sandwiches on the far banks, beyond the canal locks.

Then came the sound of an approaching motorbike. Kerry watched intently. Todd stepped out of the cabin on to the deck. His visitor was early.

The motorbike throttled into view. The rider pulled up on the track beside Todd's barge and removed his crash helmet. Kerry let out a gasp – he could hardly believe his eyes.

"Good morning, Mr Edwards," said Campbell, the team captain of *The Barons*. He ran his hand nervously through his blonde hair.

Todd smiled. "Come aboard, Captain!"

Campbell parked his bike at the side of the track, climbed on to the deck and followed Todd into the cabin. The door was slid shut.

Kerry, crouched low, waded out through the ferns and then, bent double, stole across the track. He slid down the canal bank beside the barge and immersed himself among the reeds. His new position gave him a good view of the barge, but the voices from within the closed cabin were an indistinct murmur. The three men were sitting round the cabin table drinking glasses of beer. Campbell looked uneasy. Todd, however, appeared quite jovial. The other man simply watched. Somehow, Kerry felt sure that Todd was the boss of the situation.

Then Todd opened an attaché case and took out a thick, bulging envelope. He handed it to Campbell. The team-captain hesitated before he accepted it. Finally, Campbell got to his feet and shook Todd's hand. Todd smiled and slid open the door.

Kerry scrambled up the bank, crept swiftly across the track and crawled back into his hiding place. His stomach muscles were taut with tension. He was panting thickly.

Todd watched from the deck as Campbell left the barge and crossed over to his motorbike. Campbell strapped on his helmet.

"Nice to do business with you, Captain," grinned Todd.

Campbell raised a hand as he rode away down the track. Todd turned back into the cabin and shut the door.

What a turn up, thought Kerry. His head buzzed as he lay there, awaiting further developments. The sun grew hot. An aeroplane droned distantly across the sky. Crickets chirped in the undergrowth. The canal stretched lazily between the trees.

An hour passed. The two men remained inside the cabin. Kerry glanced down at his watch. One-thirty. Dad would be missing him. Kerry looked towards the barge. Both men were sitting in their shirt sleeves, idly reading the Sunday newspapers. Nothing more was going to happen here, Kerry reckoned. Not for the moment. Get back home, he told himself. It's time you spoke to Dad.

Kerry crept back to his motorbike.

His father was in the kitchen preparing Sunday lunch when Kerry came in, and smiled uneasily. "Hello there, Kerry!" he said a little too brightly, with a false edge to his cheerful manner.

"Hello, Dad."

"Haven't seen you all morning." His father spoke pleasantly, but with a strangely unreal air.

"Went across to the practice track this morning, watched Trevor riding," said Kerry. He felt awkward and self-conscious in his father's presence. The events of the previous night still hung over them. "*The Barons* are in great form. Trev's riding really well."

"Good . . ." His father went to the sink and drained a saucepan of cauliflower.

"How are you, Dad?" Kerry asked tentatively.

"Fine," was the answer. "I'm fine."

Kerry glanced through to the living-room. He saw that the prize-cup had been replaced on the bookshelf.

"Only you seemed a bit bothered last night."

His father forced a brief laugh. "Oh, you know, one of those days when everything went wrong! Just a touch of temper, that's all!"

"Dad—" Kerry began.

"Sorry if I was a bit sharp with you, son." He took two

warm dinner plates out of the oven. "Lunch is ready."

Kerry suddenly blurted it out. "Dad, what's up with you and this bloke Todd Edwards?"

His father banged the plates down on the kitchen table. He stared at Kerry for a moment, stunned.

"It was Todd Edwards who came here last night," Kerry said.

"Listen, my lad! Just keep out of it, you understand?" His father's voice was low as he struggled to control his temper. He wagged a warning finger at Kerry. "I mean that!"

Kerry stepped forward. "What's going on, Dad?"

"Get *off*!" he shouted, his face flushed red. That same intense air of desperation had risen in him. His father turned away.

Kerry crossed quickly out of the kitchen.

Upstairs, he leaned out of his bedroom window and looked over the back yards below. He watched some kids play hopscotch in the sunlight, leaping across the squares chalked on the concrete.

What *was* going on? Kerry was utterly bewildered. He wanted to tell his father what he'd seen at the canal that morning, but it was impossible to talk to him. Maybe Kerry hadn't been tactful enough, broached it in the right way. But it was as if his father had erected a castle wall around himself and pulled up the draw-bridge. How things had changed!

Kerry thought back over the past twenty-four hours. Until then their lives had been comparatively normal. Kerry had felt as happy-go-lucky as those kids down in the yard playing hopscotch. Suddenly everything had changed. Saturday morning came, Lacey and his gang of yobs had turned up at the restaurant and then . . . *Lacey!* A sudden thought flashed through Kerry's mind.

Kerry swung round. He paced the floor, deep in thought. He had laughed when his father suggested that Lacey's motorbike raids had been organised by somebody else, somebody in the know. Now all his instincts told him Todd was behind it. But he had to be sure. He had to find Lacey. *Now!*

As he entered Weyfield, Kerry felt as if he was riding into a foreign country. In a sense he was. Barton and Weyfield had always been rival towns, and deep-rooted antipathy existed between *The Barons* and *The Warriors* stretching back many years.

Weyfield was a coastal resort like Barton, but had been badly bombed during the war. Most of the town had been rebuilt. It was ringed by new estates and towers of high-rise flats.

Kerry rode slowly through the town centre, his eyes raking the streets for Lacey. He left his bike in a car park by the war memorial hall and crossed the street to the Wimpy bar in the shopping precinct. The Wimpy was one of Lacey's regular haunts. Kerry peered in through the window. There was no sign of Lacey.

Then Kerry spotted him. He was walking into the mouth of an arcade on the opposite side of the street, alone. Kerry darted through the traffic and entered the arcade as Lacey was descending the steps at the far end.

Lacey slouched down the streets, oblivious of Kerry following close behind. Lacey turned into a long cement walk which led to one of the new estates – obviously heading for home.

The cement walk was caged in on both sides by tall link-wire fencing. Kerry was in luck. Only he and Lacey occupied the walk. He crept up behind him and clamped one hand down on Lacey's shoulder, swinging him round on his heels.

Lacey gasped in surprise. "*Ah!*—" Lacey did a double-take when he saw who it was. "*You!* You've got a nerve, Hutson, turning up here!"

"I want a word with you!"

Lacey backed away, but Kerry hedged him in against the link-wire. "What d'you want?" asked Lacey.

"I've got some questions and I want the answers."

"About what?"

"Todd Edwards."

Lacey wiped his mouth. "Never heard of him."

"I'll crack the jokes," suggested Kerry.

"I don't know what you're on about!"

Then Kerry grabbed hold of Lacey by the lapels of his leather jacket and dragged him roughly forward. "Todd Edwards! That's who I'm on about!"

Lacey looked scared. "'I've told you! . . ."

"What have you been doing in Barton, busting up places?"

"Just for laughs," whined Lacey, "bit of fun."

Kerry bounced Lacey heavily against the fence. "Come on!"

Lacey struggled. "Get off!"

"Who put you up to it?"

"No one! We—"

Kerry gripped hold of Lacey's chin and bent his head right back against the wire. "It was planned, Lacey. Regular visits. You've been coming to my old man's restaurant every week on the dot. Same with the other places in Barton." Kerry suddenly released Lacey and leaned heavily over him. "*Now!*" he shouted. "What's the set up?"

Lacey felt his neck. He stared at Kerry. "Streuth!" said Lacey, taken aback by Kerry's intensity. "What's got into you?"

Kerry was implacable. "Who's behind it, Lacey?"

"The bloke called himself Brown," Lacey said, and then fell silent.

"Let's have the rest of it!" ordered Kerry.

"Look, I can't say nothing," pleaded Lacey. "This bloke, he's dangerous. He'll have me done over, he said so!"

"He won't know. I'll keep my mouth shut."

"Why should I tell you anyway?" Lacey scowled.

"Because first you've got *me* to reckon with. *Then* the police. So out with it!"

Lacey turned away from Kerry and looked through the link-wire fence across at the rows of bungalows beyond. He spoke sullenly. "He came down from London a month back. Chatted us up."

"What does he look like?" asked Kerry.

"Tall and dark, big looking, got up smart. A right cool one," said Lacey bitterly. "He's got a mate. Fat, bald-headed little frog."

"And they drive a red Maxi?"

"Yeah, that's it. He knew who I was, this bloke, he knew all about my gang. And he said he had a job for us."

"What's the plan behind it?"

"I dunno, he didn't let on about that. Just told us what to do." Lacey shrugged and shook his head. "But he wanted your old man's place done over special. *Make sure you visit The King Cinder,* he said. *Put the boot in good and proper.*"

"Why?"

"Your old man's a big noise in Barton. I reckoned on this bloke starting up a protection racket."

"Protection racket?" Kerry said thoughtfully.

"Yeah, you know," explained Lacey, "you pay us to look after your place, or else there'll be some bother, one or two accidents. Me and the gang – we've done it round here with titchy little shops, just for a few quid. But the way this bloke was talking, sounded like it was going to be big."

"How d'you mean, *was?*"

"He's gone and put a stop to it," Lacey told him. "Last night we got paid off."

Kerry stared at Lacey in disbelief.

"Straight up," said Lacey. "*No more clobbering,* he said. That's it – *caput!* He clouted me and said if any of the gang showed up in Barton again, I'd get marked."

Kerry shook his head. "I don't get it . . ."

"You're not the only one," Lacey complained. "Maybe he's got some real heavies ready to move in. But why bother with a place like Barton?"

"There could be a reason. He comes from these parts . . ."

"I thought he came from London?"

Kerry shook his head. "He left Barton years ago."

"It still don't add up!" Lacey insisted. "Why come back here? This bloke, he's a big-timer I reckon, in with the city gangs. He's loaded!"

Kerry looked at Lacey sarcastically. "Pay you well for your work, did he?"

"Look," said Lacey, "I've told you what you wanted!"

"You didn't have any choice, so don't make it sound like you've done me a favour."

Lacey grew angry. "You caught me off guard, Hutson. Got

your own way because I weren't looking over me shoulder! Would've been different otherwise . . ."

Kerry glanced back at Lacey. "You've got off lightly, mate. You could've been in big trouble with the police. Just think yourself lucky!"

"Get stuffed!" Lacey shouted.

"You're just nothing," Kerry told him, "without your pack of bloodhounds."

"I'm going to get you for this," Lacey threatened.

Kerry shrugged. "You can try," he said as he walked away.

"I'm going to get you, Hutson!" Lacey shouted.

He watched Kerry turn out of the cement walk and disappear down the street. Lacey swung round and raced along the walk, his boots smacking loudly across the cement. He reached the estate and tore down the row of bungalows. At the end of the road, clustered round a lamp-post, were Lacey's gang.

Halfway down the pavement, Lacey stopped dead in his tracks. He pushed two fingers inside his mouth and let out a loud, shrill whistle.

6 Spider Web

Kerry rode slowly out of Weyfield, deep in thought, paying little attention to the road ahead. So his hunch had proved correct, but it set up a further series of unfathomable questions. What was the real purpose behind Todd's protection scheme? Where did Campbell, the Barton speedway captain, fit into it all? And why was his father so agitated over Todd Edwards, why was he so scared?

Something, somewhere, was very badly wrong. And his father was mixed up in it. Kerry had impetuously resolved to get to the bottom of it all. But now he was beginning to feel afraid of what he might find.

As Kerry sauntered along the scrubland track heading home towards Barton, he yawned. A sleepless night and the pressures of the day's events had tired him out. Suddenly he was conscious of being watched. He looked up. On the track ahead, hovering in a straight line across the scrubland, Lacey and his gang were waiting.

"Right!" yelled Lacey. "*Get him!*"

The motorbike pack instantaneously kicked their machines into action. A huge mechanical growl swept across the scrubland. The black riders droned forward, spreadeagled in an all-engulfing web, cutting off Kerry's immediate means of escape. They moved in swiftly. Kerry was trapped.

Kerry swung indecisively about on the track, surrounded and outnumbered by the approaching riders. The gang reached

Kerry and tore round him like terriers, sending up a bowl of dust into the air.

Lacey rode up to Kerry and grinned at him through his plastic visor. "Hello there, Hutson," he croaked.

Kerry revved hard and suddenly pitched forward, heading straight for Lacey. Lacey gulped. "What the *heck* –?" Lacey swung his bike away to avoid collision, cursing loudly as he did so. Kerry charged past him.

Kerry's sudden bolt forward took the gang by surprise. Relentlessly Kerry mowed his way through the marauding riders. As he passed them he stuck out his boot, knocking one rider to the ground, then he tore away across the scrubland.

"*After him!*" screamed Lacey.

Kerry skilfully wove his way round the gravel craters, his bike violently ripping up the gorse, stinging-nettles and couch grass which lay in its path. The straggling line of the gang roared along in pursuit. One rider tipped into a crater and went crashing down with a loud yell. Then there were only four, including Lacey, still giving chase.

Kerry had crossed over to the Barton side of the scrubland. The gang still came after him. He mounted a slope and wound his way through a maze of dead trees. Two of the riders followed. Kerry looked back, and saw one of the riders crunching heavily into the flaking tree-trunks, effectively blocking the path for his comrade. Kerry splashed loudly through a black puddle, swung to avoid a bleak stretch of rubbish dumps, and headed back down towards the track. Lacey was waiting there for him. Like a bad penny, thought Kerry.

Lacey sat astride his motorbike, hectically waving at his comrades, shouting incoherent orders through the rising dust. But the dispirited riders were limping slowly back across the scrubland towards Weyfield.

Kerry drew up beside Lacey. "It's not worth it," he told the gang-leader. "Go home, Lacey, there's a good lad." He grinned and rode on towards Barton.

Kerry sat astride his motorbike between the trees and

watched the barge. Dusk was falling. The woods were still. Curtains were drawn across the cabin windows and a light shone dimly. Jazz music echoed from the barge and drifted across the flat canal water. Kerry sat motionless, staring intently at the barge. He didn't move until darkness fell.

That night Kerry had a nightmare. Complete exhaustion had driven him into a fitful, feverish sleep. He dreamed he was swimming through the canal water after Todd. Dad had been tied to the trunk of a tree with the fat man guarding him. Trevor and Tom sat on the canal banks, watching Kerry as they sipped from tins of Coke. Lacey stood on the barge deck, laughing at Kerry. Todd was escaping, swimming swiftly down the canal. It was imperative for Kerry to stop Todd before he got away. Everything depended on it. But Kerry couldn't catch up with Todd. He swam desperately but however much he tried he couldn't move forward through the water. Then Todd stopped and stood there in the canal, the water swelling up to his neck. He leered at Kerry. Suddenly Todd's face fell away like a mask, and floated across the water. Now he wore a different face. It was Dad's.

Kerry woke up in a cold sweat. He sat up in bed. His alarm clock was ringing shrilly. It was eight o'clock, time to get ready for school. Kerry let out a sigh of relief and climbed out of bed.

Fletcher Street Comprehensive was a brand new, huge, modern building which sat incongruously at the back of the town among a maze of old terraced streets, rows of shops, factories and offices. Red-bricked and chromium-plated, glass-windows and steel-girders glinting in the morning sunlight, the building-complex looked more like a satellite space-station than a secondary school.

Kerry always gave Nikki a lift in to school on the back of his motorbike. Normally, he hated Monday mornings, but today he was glad to get back to the familiar, everyday routine. It actually felt good to arrive at school!

The playground was packed with kids and Kerry willingly allowed himself to be swallowed up in the throng. He and Nikki strolled along by some railings. Nikki noticed that Kerry was unusually quiet this morning, as if his mind was elsewhere. He seemed depressed.

Nikki nudged him. "Lovely day, then!"

Kerry looked up. "Eh . . ."

"What's up with you this morning?"

"Things on me mind," said Kerry.

"You seem a bit bothered."

"There's trouble at home," he told her. "With Dad . . ."

"What's it about?" Nikki asked.

Kerry ran his hand along the top of the railings. "I don't know. Yet . . ."

"Sometimes helps to talk," suggested Nikki. "Helps you see things."

Kerry shook his head. "Just too complicated. Don't know what it's all about myself, really."

They walked on, Kerry with his eyes cast down. "Well, come on! *Smile*!" said Nikki. She was going to do her best to buck him up. She bared her teeth at him in a mock smile.

But Kerry didn't respond. "Don't feel like smiling, thanks very much," he said self-pityingly.

"Things are never as bad as they look!"

"They look pretty bad right now," moaned Kerry.

"*Aarh*!" scoffed Nikki. "I hear the violins playing!"

"Jump off!" snapped Kerry.

"It's never as bad as you think, you know," Nikki said brightly. Kerry walked along in silence. "It's like the story of this bloke," began Nikki. "End of the world, you see, a touch of your H. G. Wells. *Pow*! Everybody dead!" Nikki grinned. "All except one little bloke in a high-rise block of flats. On his tod, last man alive on earth."

"Does this story take long?" groaned Kerry.

Nikki refused to be side-tracked. "And he can't stand the loneliness of it. *It's not on is this,* he says to himself. *I can't do with it any longer, nobody to talk to except the cat.* So he decides to end it all, do himself in."

Kerry looked at Nikki. "Hope there's a happy ending," he put in sarcastically.

Nikki continued: "He climbs right up to the top of the

high-rise and then *jump!* Chucks himself off the top-floor. Comes whizzing down . . ." Nikki gave a nose-dive whistle in illustration. "And as he's passing the fifteenth floor, you know what?"

"What?"

"He hears the telephone ringing." Nikki grinned. "Silly thing to do, weren't it?" Kerry stared at her impassively. He didn't react to the story at all. Nikki shrugged. "Probably a wrong number anyway!"

Kerry remained poker-faced. "That's quite a funny story, Nikki," he said.

"Well I thought so!" Nikki said. She was a bit cheesed off.

Kerry glanced at her. "There's only one thing."

"What's that?"

"What happened to the cat?"

Nikki stuck her tongue out at him and in spite of himself, Kerry laughed.

"Want some?" Clayton asked. He offered a thick slab of chocolate to Todd. Todd shook his head. Clayton was much relieved by Todd's refusal. "Supposed to give you energy!" Clayton chuckled as he popped the chocolate into his mouth.

Todd drove through the town centre, switching on the radio in order to drown the sound of Clayton's munching teeth. They were passing the market square.

Clayton spotted something through the window. "Hey, look at that old scouse!" He pointed out a bearded old man, dressed in a patched pullover and baggy trousers. He wore a pair of sandals several sizes too big for him, and supported himself with a walking stick.

Nulty watched the red Maxi nose up the street towards him. He recognised Todd in the driver's seat. And there was the short fat one, just as Kerry had described him, sitting next to Todd. Nulty knew that Todd would never be able to recognise him, even if he remembered him. Nulty had changed out of all recognition since his speedway days.

"Hang on, Todd," Nulty said. "Pull over to the side."

Todd frowned. "What for?"

Clayton dug into his trouser pocket and brought out a ten-penny bit. "Watch this," he smirked. "Bit of a laugh, you'll see . . ."

Todd reluctantly pulled over to the side of the road. He kept the engine running and watched Clayton, barely managing to suppress his irritation.

Clayton wrapped the coin in the silver foil from his bar of chocolate, looking up and grinning at Todd as he did so. He carefully squeezed the foil, pressing the silver into a series of neatly-edged sides round the outside of the coin, giving it an angular shape. He held it up. The coin now closely resembled a fifty-pence piece. "There!" exclaimed Clayton, proud of his workmanship. He glanced at Todd. "Watch this!"

Clayton climbed out of the car and crossed the pavement over to Nulty's stall. "Hey there, dad!" he called.

Nulty observed Clayton inscrutably. "Morning, sir," he said.

"Pound of shrimps, please," beamed Clayton.

"Shrimps it is," said Nulty cheerfully. "Thirty pence to you, sir."

Clayton took the bag of shrimps and placed the coin in Nulty's hand. Nulty began sifting through an Oxo-tin full of loose change.

"That's all right, soldier!" said Clayton, expansively. "Keep the change."

"Thank you, sir!" said Nulty.

"Buy the wife some socks," grinned Clayton.

Nulty saluted him. "Thank you very much, sir!"

Clayton climbed back into the car and peered out through the rear window as they drove off.

Nulty tossed the coin in his hand, unpeeled the foil and watched the car cruise down through the market. He would remember that clever little fat man.

Clayton roared with laughter, pointing through the rear window "*Look* at him!" he bellowed. "See his face!"

Todd gripped the steering wheel tightly. "You're an oaf, Clayton!" he barked.

Clayton's laughter quickly disintegrated into a hoarse choking sound. He looked startled. "Eh?"

Todd snatched up the bag of shrimps and flung it angrily through the window. The shrimps were scattered across the pavement. Clayton looked amazed. "What's up?" he asked tentatively.

Todd looked fiercely through the windscreen. "Here we are, in this town, on important business. And *you* think we've got all the time in the world to play games with a stupid old man!"

"Well, I didn't mean—"

"Shut up! We've got work to do."

They shot up the hill towards Old Barton, a quarter of the town which once, long ago, was the exclusive belt of the town, where only the well-to-do lived. Now it was a slum district.

It was the end of the day-shift and workers streamed out through the main gates of the light-engineering factory, a sprawling collection of pre-war grey rabbit-hutch-shaped buildings. Trevor and Tom rode their motorbikes past the straggling lines of men out to the road beyond.

"See you at the practice track tonight, Tom!" shouted Trevor above the roar of the engines. "Seven o'clock sharp!"

"OK!" waved Tom. "I'll be there!"

"Don't be late, mind!"

Trevor filtered into the thick knot of home-bound traffic and swept along, skirting outside the long queue of vehicles. Within ten minutes he was passing the gas-works and crossed the iron draw-bridge down into the docks.

He rode swiftly. Trevor loathed the dockland. Its long vacant streets populated with stray dogs. Its tall dark buildings and overhead fuel conveyors. The dingy little pubs on street corners. The metallic hammering which echoed from the yards beat down against his helmet like brick-sized hail stones. The bleak moan of foghorns across the quay depressed him.

Trevor skirted Fitzroy Park and approached the avenues of

crumbling Edwardian houses beyond. He was now riding through the heart of Old Barton.

The houses sat like rows of forgotten spinsters at a summer ball. They had long been given over to bedsitters and flats, and now the area was due for demolition. In the tall rooms leather-faced landladies with the well-rehearsed manner of world-weary debt-collectors cornered shifty tenants. Outside, along the crumbling façades, a strange silence reigned. Weeds had exploded through the concrete frontages and ivy snaked up the high walls. Trevor's motorbike echoed through the stillness.

Trevor smelt the fumes of the biscuit factory as he turned into his street. There it lay. Tonnerton Row. He looked down the tawdry street. Windows blocked up with sheets of corrugated iron. *For Sale* notices fixed to the rusty iron railings. Lines of washing stretching from window to window.

Independence from his father had cost Trevor a great deal of self respect. Every night he rode home to this dingy street. Trevor didn't have any girlfriends. Imagine bringing any girl back to Tonnerton Row! The seedy little bedsit on the top floor of number seventeen was all he could afford out of his meagre factory wages. But not for long, vowed Trevor. He avoided girlfriends for another reason. All his energy was concentrated into his prospective career: professional speedway. One day soon he would shake off the dust of Tonnerton Row for ever, wave bye-bye to Barton. He would have money in his pocket, a bird at his elbow, and a smile on his face. Then there would be no looking back. The boy from the sticks would make good. And he would do it by himself, by his own efforts, there would be no riding on his father's reputation.

Trevor pulled up outside number seventeen. He had to dismount and push his bike over the pavement across to the alleyway which ran beside the house. Somebody had parked their car across the mouth of the alleyway. A red Maxi.

Todd stood at the window watching. "Get to the door," he told Clayton. "He's on his way up."

Clayton moved to the door and hid himself in the alcove beside it.

Todd sat on the bare wooden table in the middle of the

room and lit a cigar. He appeared perfectly relaxed. He glanced casually round the bedsitter. The furniture was not new and when new had not been beautiful. A single unmade bed along one wall. An ugly gas-stove in a pokey kitchenette. A blocked-off fireplace. Peeling wallpaper. A squat wardrobe with one door swinging loose. A naked light bulb hanging from a frayed length of flex. A place for sleeping in and passing through, thought Todd. He was very familiar with bedsitting-rooms. He had lived in places like this when he was young and skint. He blew out a plume of cigar smoke and waited.

Trevor parked his bike in the wooden shed at the bottom of the alleyway. He crossed over and climbed up the fire-escape, boots clattering on the iron steps. He passed through the swing-doors and into the narrow passageway beside the row of bedsitters. The passageway smelt of disinfectant and boiled cabbage. Outside his bedsitter he pulled the latch-key from his trouser pocket, but the key jammed as he tried to push it into the lock, and the door whined open. Trevor frowned. He was always careful about locking his door whenever he went out. You could trust nobody in this neighbourhood. He pushed the door open and stepped inside.

"Hello, Trevor," Todd said. He slid off the table.

Trevor gaped in bewilderment. "*Who—?*"

"We want a word with you," Todd told him.

Suddenly the door slammed shut behind Trevor. He swung round. Clayton was leaning against the door, watching Trevor.

"How the hell did you get in here?" Trevor asked.

Todd smiled. "The caretaker was very obliging."

Kerry had to speak to somebody, had to tell someone about it all. He couldn't really expect Nulty to understand and it wasn't fair to hang himself round Nikki's neck. There was only Trevor to turn to. Kerry knew that his brother wouldn't be all that sympathetic, especially over anything connected with Dad. But Trevor's attitude might change when he heard about Todd and the secret meeting with the Barton speedway captain.

In any event, thought Kerry, at least Trevor will be somebody to talk to.

Kerry rode across the sportsground and pulled up beside Tom at the edge of the practice track. "Wotchyer there, Tom!"

"Hello, Kerry," said Tom. "What's happened to your big brother, then?"

"Trev?" Kerry glanced round. Trevor was nowhere to be seen. "Thought he'd be here." Kerry spotted Campbell, *The Barons'* captain, chatting to some of the riders by the track.

"I wanted to speak to him."

"He said he'd be here at seven," Tom said.

"It's well past eight now . . ."

"Not like Trev," said Tom. "He hasn't missed a practice session yet. Specially so close to the meeting next Sunday."

"When did you last see him?"

"Leaving work tonight."

Kerry frowned. "And he definitely said he was coming?"

"Told *me* not to be late!"

Trevor . . . Todd . . . of course, thought Kerry. Why else had Todd been watching them here at the sportsground the previous morning? And it was something to do with that Campbell over there. Kerry had the impulse to go over and smash the truth out of the team captain. Cool down, he told himself, there was probably a simple explanation of Trevor's absence. But there was only one way to find out.

Kerry pushed down his visor. "I'll go round to Trev's place," he said to Tom, "see if he's there." And he roared off.

Half-way down Tonnerton Row he screeched to a sudden halt, tipping over and almost toppling off the bike. "*Streuth!*" he gasped. So he had been right. The Maxi haunted him wherever he went. He rode slowly down to number seventeen, keeping the motorbike engine as quiet as possible. His arms and legs were stiff with tension. Maybe he should call in the police. But what would he tell them?

The curtains were drawn in Trevor's bedsitter and a light shone. Kerry pushed his bike down the alleyway, and hid it behind the wooden shed at the bottom, dumping his helmet on the saddle. He crept across the alleyway towards the foot of the fire-escape.

The swing-doors at the top sliced open. He heard a voice – Todd's voice. Kerry darted back across to the shed and crouched down, curling himself into a ball behind his motorbike.

Todd hurried down the fire-escape steps, Clayton following slowly. At the bottom he turned round and snapped impatiently: "Come on, Clayton!"

So *that* was the fat one's name, thought Kerry. He waited until he heard the car doors slam shut and the engine start up. Then he saw the car back into the alleyway and swing off down the street.

Kerry leapt up the steps of the fire-escape two at a time. *What had they done to Trevor?* Panic riddled through Kerry as he barged through the double swing-doors, colliding with a middle-aged woman carrying a large basket of laundry. He didn't stop to apologise. The woman shouted angrily after him down the passageway.

He rushed to Trevor's door, then stopped. Inside, a pop record was playing and Kerry could hear Trevor whistling to it. Kerry frowned, and banged on the door.

Trevor grinned broadly. "Kerry! What you doing here?" He swung back the door and Kerry stepped inside.

"Just dropped by."

"You look a bit puffed. Want some coffee?"

"Ta." Kerry watched his brother fill the kettle, light a gas-jet and plonk the kettle on top. "Passed two blokes as I came in," Kerry said casually. "They drove off in a red Maxi. Seen them around at all?"

Trevor had his back to Kerry. "Nope. Why?"

Kerry went over and sat on the bed. "Just wondered. Couldn't see them living in a place like this. They looked too posh."

Trevor was silent. He was measuring out instant coffee into two chipped mugs.

"You didn't get down to the practice track tonight, then?" asked Kerry.

"*Practice*!" scoffed Trevor. "Who needs it? Not against crumby Weyfield!"

Something caught Kerry's eye. He noticed a thick, bulging envelope lying on top of Trevor's bedside table. It was unsealed, and contained a roll of five-pound notes wound with an elastic band. Slowly, Kerry looked up at his brother.

Trevor grinned at Kerry. "Well, kid," he said, "it's been quite a day!"

Kerry watched him impassively. "Yeah? You sound cheerful. Won the pools or something?"

He had never seen Trevor in such good humour. "Going out for a drink with the lads later on," Trevor said. "Bit of a celebration."

"Celebration?"

Trevor rubbed his hands together enthusiastically. "*Yep!* Our captain—"

"What about him?"

"Campbell is retiring from the team." The kettle on the gas-stove began whistling. "And you're the very first to know, kid," said Trevor. "I'm the new captain!"

Kerry wanted to shout at Trevor, yell at him. But he couldn't move a muscle. He just sat there on the bed, frozen inside, feeling like a zombie. "Great news, hey?" laughed Trevor. "I'll be leading *The Barons* against Weyfield next Sunday . . ."

The kettle whistled shrilly as it came to the boil. The sound echoed through Kerry's mind like someone screaming.

7 Speedway

Kerry watched through the classroom window. Outside rain pelted down so hard it was as if someone had just turned on a giant cold-water tap full blast. Water tumbled along the gutters and overflowed, cascading on to the tarmac below. The rain swept across the cycle sheds, the school hall and the caretaker's house. The sportsfield belly-danced with overflowing puddles. The classroom blocks across the courtyard looked tall in the rain.

Two teachers ran across the courtyard, soaked to the skin. Kerry smiled to himself. That was the only good thing that had happened all week. It was Friday afternoon. In a couple of hours school would be over and the weekend stretched before Kerry. Normally Kerry looked forward to weekends. But not this one.

Nothing much had happened since Kerry visited Trevor in his bedsitter on Monday night. Trevor assumed the role of team captain as if he were born to it. Dad remained obstinately silent, and still rejected any of Kerry's attempts to discover what had occurred on Saturday. Todd and Clayton stayed on their barge and hadn't ventured into Barton all week, so far as Kerry knew. He checked with Nulty a couple of times. Nulty told him about the incident with the faked coin, but since then there had been no sign of the men in town. Life went on normally. It was as if Kerry had dreamed all the events he had witnessed. As if his suspicions were merely the product of a vivid imagination. But Kerry knew that this truce was a temporary one. Very soon now Todd's machinations would begin again. Todd was waiting for Sunday to come when *The Barons* would ride against *The Warriors* at Barton Stadium and Trevor receive his public baptism as team captain. What might happen after that, Kerry dreaded to think.

Today we have naming of parts. The class were reciting a poem in unison. It was in preparation for the school concert at the end of term. *Yesterday we had daily cleaning and tomorrow morning we shall have what to do after firing.* The collective voice droned on. Nikki glanced across the classroom and saw Kerry staring out at the rain sheeting against the window. He's got them again, thought Nikki, a touch of the moody blues. *But today, today we have naming of parts.* Kerry had been like this all week. He was being a real pain. No matter how many times Nikki asked, Kerry wouldn't tell her what the matter was. Maybe he was fed up with her and didn't have the courage to finish things. Well, Nikki could take a hint! If that was the way Kerry wanted it, then fine by her. Nikki's scalp suddenly began itching. *Japonica glistens like coral in all of the neighbouring gardens, and today we have naming of parts . . .*

"Nikki Stevens," warned Miss Fuller, the school mistress presiding, "girls who scratch their heads will get splinters in their fingers!"

"Yes, miss . . ." Nikki replied sourly. Her head still itched.

They caught the bus home. The rain had been too heavy that day to use Kerry's motorbike. Kerry sat there, hunched up in the corner of the seat. Nikki sat beside him, watching a fly crawl across the roof of the bus. If he's got anything to say, thought Nikki, then let the oracle speak first. She was staying quiet.

Finally, Kerry nodded out the window. "Wonder how long this will keep up?" he said flatly.

"*Oh!*" Nikki cocked her head at him. "Thought you'd caught a cold and lost your voice today!"

"Got things on my mind," Kerry grumbled.

"Then go and write a poem about it," Nikki advised. She was in no mood to offer sympathy.

The rain pounded down on the roof. After a moment, Kerry said: "I'm not riding down the fairground tomorrow night, giving it a rest this weekend." He looked at Nikki. "So I'll see you Sunday afternoon."

"Will you?"

"At the speedway. You're going to come?"

"Want me to?" Nikki's voice was curt.

"Course I do!"

Nikki looked away. "I wasn't so sure!"

"Yes," Kerry said quietly, "I want you to come."

Kerry sat in his bedroom most of Saturday staring out at the driving rain. Lightning flashed and distant thunder rolled. Maybe they'll have to cancel the Barton-Weyfield meeting if this weather keeps up, he thought. He hoped they would, though he wasn't sure what eventual difference it would make. Anything to disrupt Todd's plans . . .

But even the weather sided with Todd. It stopped raining during the night, and by Sunday morning the clouds had gone. There was a fine drizzle which cleared by lunchtime. A long, sad rainbow hung in the sky over Barton. The wet streets glistened in the brilliant sunshine.

The Salvation Army band played for three-quarters of an hour in the centre of Barton Stadium before the racing began. As *Rock of Ages* drifted across the muddy shale surface of the circular track, the fans filled the stands. About three thousand supporters turned up at each race meeting. They flooded in through the main gates of the stadium, enthusiastically lining up for tickets and buying speedway magazines and newspapers sold from stands dotted around the stadium. There was a hushed air of anticipation among the fans.

Kerry usually relished the atmosphere of speedway, quite apart from the tension and excitement of the racing. It was even better when the meetings used to be held on Wednesday nights, then you got the magnetic thrill of watching the riders circle the track by floodlight. Night-time racing brought an edge of danger to the spectacular. Now the Wednesday night spot had been given over to greyhound racing and speedway relegated to Sundays. But the day-time atmosphere was still intoxicating. Eager crowds were gathered round hot-dog and coffee stalls. A long queue waited for hot chestnuts roasting over furnace-red braziers. Kids avidly read their speedway fan magazines. Rival groups of supporters chanted slogans at one another. The family groups who had attended speedway regularly for decades, sometimes coming from miles away, reunited once again and hurriedly began exchanging gossip. The coach loads of supporters, many of them already drunk and singing wildly, fought for seats in the grandstand. Kerry normally submerged himself in the electric excitement of the event – speedway was a home from home for him. But today was different.

He and Nikki stood among the crowds packed like sardines in the standing-room area. This was beside barricades at the side of the track and behind thick wire netting, but you got a good view of the racing for a ticket much cheaper than for a grandstand seat. And close to the track, you felt the raw, immediate impact of the racing. As the motorbikes skidded round the bend, hot shale would spit up from the track into the standing crowds. Kerry loved to feel the warm specks of clay brush against his face as he stood there, crushed in the throng, cheering wildly among them. But not today.

Nikki had brought a copy of the local speedway club's fan magazine. It was a fairly amateur-looking publication, duplicated, with the pages stapled loosely together. On the front cover, there was a large profile of Trevor's head and shoulders, and his lavish signature adorned the illustration. A caption read: *Trevor Hutson – The New King Cinder!* Nikki nudged Kerry and pointed out the magazine. Kerry stared at it for a moment and then looked stiffly away across the track. The Salvation Army band had stopped playing and was being clapped out of the stadium. After a moment, piped music of the kind they play in airport lounges, filtered through the loud-speakers. Racing was due to begin in ten minutes.

In the pits, both teams were preparing themselves for the racing. Riders for *The Barons* isolated themselves from members of *The Warriors*. Many riders were doing some last-minute tinkering to their motorbikes. Some sat upon their bikes, revving up the engines. Others strapped their helmets on.

The Barons wore red, white and blue, with the emblem of a gloved fist on the front of their rubber tunics and on the bridge of their helmets. *The Warriors* were in black and gold. Most riders attempted to maintain a blasé front. But there were those constant wise cracks and edgy jokes which revealed a deep tension between the two teams.

Trevor and Tom were ready, sitting astride their motorbikes, about to ride out on to the track. Trevor was quite nervous.

"Got the colly wobbles?" grinned Tom.

"I'll be all right."

"Course you will! Best of luck, Trev!"

Trevor grinned. "And you, Tom!"

They both roared out of the pits towards the track.

Kerry had been watching the grandstand intensely. Then he spotted them. Gradually making their way along a row of seats, with people standing up to let them pass. Todd was carrying the field-glasses. Clayton wore a cloth cap. They reached two seats at the centre. The best in the grandstand. Campbell, the ex-captain, was nowhere to be seen. Lacey and his gang, usually here on the terraces making trouble, were also absent.

The piped music faded. Four speedway riders roared along the track towards the starting grids. The surrounding crowds let out a huge cheer, Kerry standing silently amongst them. Todd raised the field-glasses to his eyes.

The four riders lined up at the tapes, ready for the first race. Trevor was positioned on the inside lane.

The loudspeaker announcements had begun. ". . . home meeting between *The Barons* of Barton . . ." A loud cheer went up from the Barton supporters . . ." and our neighbours, *The Weyfield Warriors* . . ." more cheering. The voice crackled on over the loudspeakers: "Riding for the first time as Captain of *The Barons* . . . Trevor Hutson!" Trevor raised his arms above his head. " . . . son of our own famous King Cinder, Richard Hutson . . . following in his father's footsteps . . . good luck, Trevor!" The crowd clapped and cheered rapturously. Kerry felt his stomach turn. He looked across at Todd in the grandstand. Todd lowered the field-glasses and handed them to Clayton.

The crowds were growing restless, waiting impatiently for the racing to begin. The loudspeaker voice droned on: "... riding with him in the first race, Tom Arnold of *The Barons* ... and for Weyfield ..." Clayton clutched the field-glasses to his eyes and focused the lens upon the four riders. " ... Jeff Maynard, Captain of *The Warriors* and riding with him in the first race, Dave Sutcliffe ... good luck lads!"

The crowds buzzed in tense anticipation as the four riders revved up their engines and hunched themselves over their machines, poised ready for the first race. The tapes suddenly shot up above the heads of the riders. Instantly they tore off, slicing through the muddy shale, grinding along the track in an even line. The crowds howled their support, their cheering drowned by the loud wail of angry engines.

Nikki bit the skin off a luke-warm chestnut as she watched Kerry standing beside her, totally silent amongst the noisy crowds, coldly eyeing the race meeting, his fists thrust deep into his denim pockets. She held out the bag of chestnuts. "Want one?" Kerry shook his head.

The first heat went easily to *The Barons*. Trevor was on top form and he was spurred on by the intense good will of the Barton supporters. He was flagged down at the finishing line to wild acclaim from the crowd, and Tom pulled in second. It was an impressive opening win for Barton.

The next few heats followed a similar pattern. It looked as if it would be Barton's day. The Weyfield riders looked dispirited and their supporters began shouting abuse at them. *The Barons* had the advantage of being on home ground, but the change of captaincy had enlivened the team with a vital new spirit and energy. The loudspeaker buzzed with victory results for Barton. In the midst of all this, Kerry felt like a traitor. He must have been the only Barton supporter in the stadium who wanted *The Barons* to lose.

Each time a Barton rider careered in first past the finishing line, enthusiastic groups of supporters held up huge placards with BARTON!! daubed on them in thick yellow paint.

After ten heats, *The Barons* were leading by twenty points. With only three heats left to follow, it looked as if Barton would be the victors.

The eleventh heat saw two Weyfield riders hopelessly attempting to gain ground on Trevor and Tom, who sped neck and neck round the final lap. As they both approached the finishing line, Tom revved his engine and crept past Trevor, just managing to overtake him. Trevor roared in second. He pulled up beside Tom. "I'll give you that one, Tom!"

"Jump off!" laughed Tom, rubbing off the sticky mud plastering his face.

They both watched the next heat from the pits. Jeff Maynard, captain of *The Warriors*, had the edge over the two Barton riders. Weyfield took the twelfth heat. A huge placard marked WEYFIELD!! in large red lettering rose above a crowd of Weyfield supporters.

"*Blast!*" Tom cursed under his breath.

"Doesn't matter," Trevor told him with calm self-assurance. "We're nearly home and dry." Only four heats had so far gone to Weyfield.

The final heat was announced. Trevor and Tom rode slowly out of the pits towards the grids.

"Here we go then, mate," said Trevor. "Number thirteen . . ."

Tom winked. "Unlucky for some!"

But it wasn't bad luck that dogged Weyfield. Even Kerry had to admit that his brother excelled on the track that afternoon. Nobody could touch Trevor, he was a son of the track, undisputed hero of the day. As Trevor roared home to victory for Barton, an overwhelming sense of desolation swept over Kerry. Trevor was in league with Todd Edwards and had walked that crooked mile to the captaincy of *The Barons*. Yet Trevor didn't *need* help from Todd or anyone else, his dazzling display of skill that afternoon proved it! If only things had been different! What a fantastic day this could have been . . . Kerry so thrilled . . . Dad so proud . . .

The Barons, led by Trevor, rode in a victory parade around the track. The crowd roared its applause. The loudspeaker voice hummed above the din: "It's *The Barons! . . . The*

Barons! . . . *The Barons* of Barton win! . . . led by their new captain, Trevor Hutson . . . well done, Trevor, and congratulations . . ." Then victory music was broadcast loudly over the speakers.

Kerry pushed his way through the tightly-packed, cheering crowds. Nikki followed, frowning. She was totally thrown by Kerry's weird behaviour. She lost sight of Kerry on a couple of occasions as she weaved through the crowds. Then she spotted him at a hot-dog stall, and walked over. Kerry handed her a hot-dog.

"Ta!" she said. Nikki glanced at him. "You all right, then?"

Kerry shrugged. "Yeah, why not?"

"Enjoying yourself?"

"Yeah," he said evasively.

"Having a ball?" Nikki persisted wryly.

Kerry glanced at her. "What you on about?" he asked, as if he didn't know only too well.

"Usually you're yelling y'head off down here, cheering on *The Barons.* Not a peep out of you today!"

Kerry bit into his hot-dog. He said nothing.

Nikki stared at him. "Thought you would've gone berserk, with your brother out there riding like a champ." Her voice suddenly took on an accusing tone: "What's wrong with you?"

Kerry brushed swiftly past her and walked back towards the crowds. He knew what Nikki was thinking, but how could he explain any of it to her?

The most popular event of the afternoon was yet to come. This was a knockout competition between riders of both teams. It was usually sponsored by a local firm, who put up the prize money, generally around two hundred pounds. There were four initial heats, out of which eight riders graduated to a two-heat semi-final. The four finalists then competed in one last heat for the jackpot. This was an individual event, open to all the riders in competition with one another irrespective of which club they rode for. The contest was a marvellous opportunity for riders to demonstrate their individual prowess. Most people expected Trevor to win.

During the interval, Todd and Clayton sat in silence, as

piped music whispered through the loudspeakers. Todd remembered this stadium, and the weekday meetings when he was a kid. Todd recalled gate-crashing many a meeting with his gang of mates, hooting with derision at the mud-coated riders. Hero of the day was the clean-cut Richard Hutson, king of the cinder track. Nowadays the track was laid with shale. Todd smiled with self-satisfaction. Times had changed . . .

Speedway wasn't really Clayton's scene. He preferred the horses. He had tried dropping off for a snooze, but the racing and the enthusiasm had proved too rowdy, even for Clayton. He couldn't very well retire outside to the car. Todd expected him to be there.

The piped music faded and the fans moved back to the stands. Most people had stayed for the knockout competition, though some disappointed Weyfield supporters had gone home. Kerry felt like leaving the stadium, but some strange compulsion kept him there. He glanced at Nikki. She was ignoring him. Obviously she'd given him up as a bad job.

The announcer's voice crackled across the loudspeakers: "Round Two, ladies and gentlemen . . . an individual knockout competition between the riders of both teams . . . the prize money offered this week . . . wait for it . . . *five hundred pounds!* The sponsor of the competition . . . Mr Todd Edwards of London . . ." Kerry's eyes shot up to the grandstand. "Many sincere thanks to Mr Edwards for his generous donation . . ."

Todd lit a cigar. He had been amused by the reaction of the speedway administrators. They certainly remembered Todd, his past reputation lived on in Barton. They judged him a reformed character, indeed he was obviously a man who had made a success out of life, despite everything. But they still didn't like him nor want any part of him. It had been particularly gratifying, therefore, when they suddenly warmed to Todd after he offered to put up the prize money.

Trevor and Tom both survived the first heats and the ensuing semi-finals and were to meet two Weyfield riders in the final, deciding heat.

Todd watched through the field-glasses. The four riders were lined up at the grids, revving their engines, poised ready. The loudspeaker announcement hushed the crowd: "Final heat of the knockout competition . . . the riders . . . Dave Sutcliffe, Weyfield, Tom Arnold, Barton, Jeff Maynard, Weyfield, and last but by no means least Trevor Hutson of Barton!" A loud cheer went up as Trevor's name was broadcast. He was the clear favourite. The announcer said: "Good luck lads . . . and may the best man win!" Spectators yelled out Trevor's name and stamped their feet on the wooden boards of the grandstand.

Suddenly the tapes were lifted and they were off. The four front wheels slithered through the mud, the engines spat and growled in an intense crossfire, and the riders pitched their bikes round the circuit in a fury of speed. For the first lap they were level pegging, each man trying desperately to edge forward. They tore past the barricades, drowning the hoarse shouts of their fans. Todd watched sedately from his grandstand seat, like a circus ringmaster.

The bikes belched forward, the riders piling heavily round the corners, attempting to crowd each other out. They swung down low, throwing their weight on to one side, pulling their machines down with them so that they travelled at an extreme angle, close down to the hot mud, swinging up as they met the bend, suddenly rearing like wild horses. They zig-zagged forward in a haphazard line, like wanton tearaways, their faces coated with mud and sweat, their bikes gouging up the track.

An ugly screech scarred the air. Tom. His bike twisted, and broke into a long skid, violently buckling out of control. It slid swiftly away from under him. The crowds let out a huge, communal "*OOH!*" Tom crashed to the ground, his bike sending up an explosion of shale. He somersaulted over and rolled away across the mud towards the barricade. The three remaining riders swept on around the track, oblivious of Tom's fall.

Tom appeared unharmed and picked himself up from the track and began dusting himself down. He ran over to his bike, lifted it by the handlebars, wheeled it away to the barricade, and watched the remainder of the race from there.

Trevor and the Weyfield captain, Jeff Maynard, were riding level with one another, roaring along side by side, very close.

Sutcliffe, the second Weyfield rider, followed close behind.

Kerry watched intently. Despite everything, he willed his brother to win. He couldn't remain mealy-mouthed and detached, whatever the logical justification, and he gripped the wire-netting and shouted for Trevor.

The race was now between Trevor and Maynard, who still rode neck and neck. Sutcliffe, now struggling far behind, had virtually given up.

Todd watched tensely through the field-glasses. "The final lap coming up," he told Clayton. Clayton was glad.

Trevor and Maynard were still level pegging when they clamoured noisily forward on to the final lap. It was still anyone's race. Then Trevor ground forward, minutely overtaking the Weyfield rider. The front wheel of Trevor's motorbike edged forward just ahead of Maynard's bike. They both took the corner. Trevor twisted his bike in towards Maynard, crowding him over to the side of the track, forcing him to slow down in order to avoid collision. Trevor finally overtook Maynard as they both careered round the bend towards the finishing line.

Trevor roared along the final straight. He pitched past the finishing line and was flagged down. The cheering of the crowds swelled up across the ground to him.

"He's done it!" said Todd.

Trevor rode along the track, both arms raised above his head as the crowds cheered him. Then he pulled up, sitting on his stationary bike with the engine still running, grinning broadly at his fans.

The announcer said: "And it's Trevor Hutson . . . winner of the knockout competition, Trevor Hutson, ladies and gentlemen! Congratulations Trevor . . . a well-deserved win . . . and don't spend it all at once!" The manager of *The Barons* walked out across the track and presented the prize money to Trevor. Loud victory music played through the speakers and Trevor rode a final lap of honour.

"Right," said Todd. "Let's go."

Kerry watched Todd and Clayton stand and leave their seats, moving gradually along the row of cheering spectators.

Kerry thought of following them, but he had Nikki with him. Besides, he was pretty certain he knew where they were headed.

Trevor slowly circled the track in a solo victory parade, his helmet removed and sitting on the handlebars. He was grinning broadly, and rode with one arm raised in acknowledgement of Barton's acclaim.

After the speedway meeting, the Barton team and some of their fans celebrated in *The Pits*, a pub across the road from the stadium. Singing echoed loudly through the open doors of the public bar.

Kerry rode out of the stadium car park with Nikki on the pillion. He pulled up outside the pub and peered in. Trevor was being carried shoulder-high round the bar. Everyone was singing *For He's A Jolly Good Baron!* to the accompaniment of a piano. Trevor was laughing hysterically.

Nikki dug Kerry in the ribs. "Why don't we go in there?" she asked. "Celebrate with them?" Kerry sat on the bike, silent. "It's your brother's big night – come on!" Kerry didn't move. "We'd get served, we've passed for eighteen before." Kerry watched Trevor inside the pub, loudly buying everyone a round of drinks, including the pretty barmaid. "Look," suggested Nikki, "I can get home by myself if you want to go in alone . . ." Kerry shook his head and swung the handlebars away from the kerb. Nikki quickly put her arms around him, arresting his move, linking her hands together against his chest and locking Kerry to her. She whispered confidentially in his ear. "Hey," she smiled, "you're not *jealous* of Trev, are you?"

Kerry suddenly wrenched his arms outward and broke free of Nikki's grip. Nikki gasped. "*Kerry!*"

Kerry revved up and the bike shot away from the kerb down the road. The drunken singing drifted after them until Kerry turned the bike into the next street. He roared down the council row and pulled up outside Nikki's home, keeping the engine running. Nikki climbed off and stood on the pavement by the bike, staring at Kerry.

Kerry looked straight ahead, avoiding Nikki's eyes. "OK?" he asked. He was suddenly anxious to get away.

"Kerry . . ."

Kerry glanced at her. "Pick you up in the morning," he said quickly.

"What's got into you?" Nikki wanted to know.

"Nothing . . ."

"Is it me?" she asked suddenly. Kerry shook his head firmly. "Look," said Nikki, "come on, let's have it!"

"No," Kerry told her, "nothing like that."

Nikki looked relieved. "Come indoors and have some coffee then."

Kerry turned the bike from the kerb. He had to get home. "Must get back," he said.

"Go on, *tell* me," insisted Nikki. "What's *wrong*?"

"I don't know exactly," Kerry said stiffly.

"Something over Trevor and the speedway?" Nikki hazarded a guess.

Kerry suddenly revved and shouted back at Nikki over the roar of the engine: "I'll see you in the morning!" He turned and roared swiftly off.

Nikki watched him. Right, she decided, that's *it.* She and Kerry were finished.

8 Bad Blood

Kerry wasn't at all surprised when he saw the red car parked sleekly beside the restaurant. He expected it to be there. He had guessed that Todd would pay his father a visit that night. He could see a light shining in the living-room and three figures silhouetted against the closed curtains. Now, at last, he would find out what it was all about. He stole down the lane to the back door.

The kitchen was in darkness but the murmur of angry voices came from the living-room. Kerry couldn't hear clearly what was being said. A thin strand of moonlight guided him across the kitchen to the living-room door. He eased himself up on the table, slid across it to the wall, and listened. Still the voices came as a blur of sound. Kerry carefully eased open one of the doors by two or three inches. A thin trickle of light grazed against his face.

He heard Todd's crisp, bland voice: "You didn't watch your son ride as captain of *The Barons* this afternoon?"

"No." His father's voice was sombre.

"You knew Trevor had been made captain?"

"Kerry told me."

Peering through the tiny gap, Kerry could see his father and Todd standing in the middle of the living-room, facing each other. Clayton leant against a nearby wall.

"Trevor was a great success today," Todd said. "Indeed, he surpassed my greatest expectations."

"*Your* expectations?"

There was a pause. "I put him there, Hutson," Todd said. "I fixed it so that Trevor was made captain of *The Barons*."

His father stared at Todd in disbelief. "But Campbell . . . Campbell retired!"

Todd slowly shook his head. "No, no. I'm afraid not. Tell him, Clayton."

Clayton spoke flatly, automatically, as if he were reading a report. "Campbell was bought off. Your kid's been in line to be made captain for quite a while, so the team-manager didn't need much persuading. The five-hundred pound prize-money Todd offered to put up for the knockout contest this afternoon – that also helped." Clayton ran his tongue across his fat, red lips. "And now young Trevor is on Todd's payroll," he added.

"You . . . you're . . ." his father mumbled, lost for words.

"That's the picture, Hutson," Todd assured him.

"My son would never get mixed up with the likes of you!"

"Trevor is very ambitious. And *I'm* setting him up."

"You're a liar!"

Todd spoke toughly. "Hutson, I've got your son in my pocket!"

His father pulled his jacket off the back of a chair. "I'll go and see him right now!"

"He'll say nothing," Todd told him. "Be sensible, Hutson! Trevor knows he's on to a good thing. With my connections, I can get him into the big league. And that's where he wants to be! Trevor will one day inherit your mantle." Todd smiled. "King Cinder . . ."

There was silence. His father stared at Todd intently. "What's all this in aid of, Edwards?" he asked quietly.

"I want this town paying me protection money," Todd said. "Starting with *you*."

"Your pound of flesh . . ."

Todd smiled and spoke calmly. "Hutson, I'm going to get this town right under my thumb. I'm going to squeeze Barton dry."

"It's *me*, isn't it? It's me you really want to get back at!"

Todd stared at him. "Yes, Hutson, you're right. It's you . . ."

"All right, if that's the way you want it! But why didn't you come out fighting fair and square instead of all this double-dealing?"

"To get you exactly where I wanted you. I needed Trevor on my books to really corner you."

Kerry twisted round on the table to get a better view. The exchange had confirmed all his suspicions. But he couldn't understand why his father had let Todd get this far. Why hadn't he simply called in the police? A big chunk of the jigsaw was still missing.

"What makes you think you've got me cornered?" asked his father, in a gruff, angry voice.

"Oh, you'll co-operate now, Hutson," Todd said confidently.

"Don't be so sure!"

"Then watch your own son disgraced. Not to mention yourself . . ."

"Maybe I can live with it."

Todd made an expansive gesture. "But imagine those headlines! The son of Richard Hutson becomes speedway captain by bribery." Todd paused and then added: "And very quickly it will emerge as fact that *you*, all those years ago, got to the top in exactly the same way."

Kerry bit into his tongue. He suddenly felt sick. The voices from the living-room echoed in his head, as if he were hearing them from the end of a long tunnel.

"I was a kid full of big ideas," he heard his father say. "I got conned into it."

Todd's voice whispered like the distant breeze. "Try telling that to the people in this town . . ."

"It happens to be true. I was young, short of money, gullible. Easy prey for crooked operators like you!"

"Exactly," agreed Todd. "And so with Trevor. History repeats itself. Like father like son. That's what people will say . . ."

Kerry looked away. He could no longer stand the sight of his father. He sat on the table, leaning stiffly against the wall, his whole body set, frozen into place, as if he were powerless to move.

In the living-room, his father rounded on Todd. "*You* set Trevor up by bribery. If any of this comes out, you'll get caught in the same trap."

Todd shook his head. "Oh, no. Sorry. I'll be long gone, back to the city, down into one of my holes."

"Where you belong!"

Todd laughed, a long harsh laugh. "Maybe so," he said. "Only none of that will happen, will it? You may well be prepared to see yourself ruined, you might swallow that. But not your son . . ."

There was no reply. Todd continued: "So let's get down to business. All you have to do is pay up regularly. And convince your fellow proprietors that they are in need of a little protection."

Kerry heard Todd's voice, it buzzed through his head, but no emotion registered in him. His mind gathered the information automatically, like a computer. Todd was saying: "One hundred pounds, I believe, is the amount I originally proposed. Each and every week. Yes?"

"Yes . . ." His father spoke in a humiliated, defeated voice.

"And your fellow tradesmen?"

"*Yes!*" It was almost a whisper.

"Good," said Todd. "I'll take the first instalment now. In cash, of course."

"I haven't any money here on the premises."

Todd lost his temper. His hand flew up and struck Kerry's father across the side of the face. "Don't play stupid games with me, Hutson," Todd breathed.

Kerry's father crossed over to the bookcase. Behind one shelf, built into the wall, was a small safe. He twisted the lock combination, swung the safe door open, and took out a batch of ten-pound notes.

Kerry stiffly eased himself off the kitchen table. He walked slowly, limply, as if in a trance, down the passageway into the hall.

"Clayton will be calling on your fellow proprietors within the next few days," Todd said. "So I trust you'll get busy talking to them."

"I can only suggest it to them." Kerry's father spoke in a drained, exhausted voice.

"You'll *tell* them!" ordered Todd. "Or take the consequences."

"All right . . ." Kerry heard his father say.

The voices followed Kerry like the echoes of excited ghosts as he doggedly plodded up the stairs. He gripped the banisters, suddenly dizzy. He pushed his way into his bedroom and closed the door. He deliberately didn't switch on the light. It wasn't that he was afraid of being discovered, but he wanted to be alone in the shadows, to hide away in the dark. He stood there, in the dusky light of the room, staring at the speedway posters on the walls. From the street below came the slam of car doors, and an engine stuttered into life. Kerry peered from behind the curtains, and saw the red car pull away and move off swiftly. He wondered vaguely what his father was doing, but he didn't really care.

He lay on top of the bed and waited for it to get dark. The looming pale orange reflection of street lamps shone against the walls and across the ceiling. Kerry watched the shifting patterns and made the faces of clowns out of the shapes. The back of his head throbbed against the cool pillow. The banshee wail of a police-car siren echoed across the back of the town. Kerry heard a young couple walking along the street outside. Laughing intimately, with not a care in the world, their footsteps smacked along the pavement as they hurried home. The church clock struck eleven.

He heard his father coming up the stairs, moving slowly, awkwardly, like a drunken man. He heard him go into the bathroom, then into his bedroom and slam the door shut. Kerry listened to him moving clumsily about. Something fell to the floor and smashed, and his father cursed violently. After a while, the house fell silent.

The street lights outside dimmed and only a stray finger of moonlight prodded the back of the door. Kerry climbed off the bed and looked out of the window. The lights across the town were dying, smouldering dimly in the darkness, like fire embers. Barton was asleep. He moved to his door and crept through the house, out into the night.

Kerry walked. Straight down the pavements, on through the town. Boots chopping heavily on the flagstones. Heading nowhere in particular. Just walking. Keep going. Don't stop. Don't think. Moving blindly through the night, like a desperate man. He broke into a run, a hard long sprint, his heels swacking like bullets. Ease up, you'll wake somebody. Who *cares*?

He walked on, his face bright with sweat. Slowly life was beginning to ebb back through him as the shock of the past few hours subsided. He approached a block of flats. Two pints of milk stood on a doorstep. Kerry stared at the bottles, then picked up one of the pints and tossed it in his hand. Suddenly he gripped the bottle by its neck, and flung it against the high brick wall next to the flats. The bottle crashed against the wall, and he watched the milk billow in a cascading pattern, creaming downwards, staining the brick.

The window of a top floor flat opened and a man leaned out. He looked up and down the street below, but nobody stirred. Kerry had gone.

Kerry made his first conscious decision so far that night, and headed for Seaview, a hilltop park which overlooked the town. He passed the silent railway yard, crossed a footbridge, and stepped down the road. Suddenly a hot, bright spotlight pressed against the back of his neck. Kerry twisted round, blinded by the dazzling light thrown by the two discs of car headlights. *Todd!* He shielded his eyes with his arms, trying to orientate himself, backing away across the pavement. If he tried to run, then the car would soon swoop along after him. There seemed no escape. But what could Todd want with him? Then Kerry saw a uniformed police constable climb out, carrying a torch. He looked Kerry over. "Been hanging about the streets long?"

"I live near here," Kerry volunteered.

"I didn't ask you that," said the policeman. Kerry stared at him peevishly. "What are you up to, lad?"

"Walking."

"Walking where?"

Kerry shrugged. "Just walking."

"What's the matter, can't you sleep?" The policeman shone the torch in Kerry's face. "Lost your voice, lad?"

"Took a stroll, that's all. Free country, ain't it?"

The policeman pointed the end of the torch. "Don't get fresh with me, lad. It's nearly four in the morning. That's no time to be taking your constitutional."

"Just come from my girlfriend's place," Kerry said with a blush.

"Oh, I see. Well, now. Pity you didn't stay with her." The policeman took out a notebook from his tunic pocket. "What's your name?"

"Hutson . . . Kerry Hutson." A name he was once proud of, now mumbled out of the corner of his mouth. He was asked to repeat it.

"Address?" Kerry told him. The policeman smiled at Kerry. His whole attitude suddenly changed. "You're one of Dick Hutson's sons, are you? You should've said so, first off." The policeman put his notebook away. "Well, that's all right. Best get off home, son, or your dad will worry."

The policeman climbed back into his vehicle. Kerry watched the car cruise away.

Kerry sat on a bench in Seaview Park and watched the dawn break over Barton. He felt wide awake, despite his lack of sleep. The morning chorus resounded through the trees and bushes. Dew hugged the long grass and flowers. A stream bubbled and gushed. Clouds moved mysteriously, interweaving like mime dancers, unfolding the sky. The pale mask of the sun appeared, a faint circle stencilled on the horizon. An early morning train left the station, snaking out across the countryside. A bus growled through Kitchener estate, picking up queues of workmen.

There *had* to be mitigating circumstances, thought Kerry. That was the only explanation. His father was trying to protect somebody, or he was laying some kind of trap for Todd.

Kerry began to feel a little better as this idea gained strength in his mind. Was it really possible that his own father was a crook? In his heart of hearts, Kerry knew that he could no longer be sure. He just had to give him the benefit of the doubt, for the moment at least.

But then there was Trevor. There could be no mitigation for him, even though he obviously couldn't be aware that Todd was using him as a pawn. What a mess! And there was one man responsible for it: Todd Edwards.

Kerry knew that he had to go and see Trevor. *Now*, before things got even worse. But Kerry wasn't at all sure that he could face his brother without a punch-up quickly following. Yet he *had* to explain how Todd was using Trevor to blackmail Dad. Then Trevor would cut off his association with Todd and that would finish Todd's game. So, despite his hatred of the whole business, he must talk to Trevor, and the sooner the better.

Kerry caught a double-decker bus to Old Barton. It was packed with workmen carrying lunch tins and women office cleaners with grey, tired faces. The passengers rode in silence, reading their newspapers. Kerry studied the passing rows of houses. Monday morning. People leaving home, on their way to work. Ordinary individuals, with commonplace, mundane routines. Kerry envied them. He longed to get back to a normal, straightforward way of life. He wondered if it would ever be possible again.

Kerry got off the bus at the corner of Tonnerton Row. He followed the postman down the street to number seventeen. The time was seven-thirty.

Two cats sat on the dustbins lining the alleyway, moaning and spitting as they worked themselves up into a scrap. Kerry peered in through the window of the shed and saw Trevor's bike inside. He crossed over to the fire-escape and ran up the steps. Trevor's bedsitter door stood ajar and thick snoring came from within the room.

Trevor was slumped across his bed, fully dressed, in a heavy sleep. He still wore his sports jacket. His collar and a few buttons of his shirt were undone. Kerry stood at the side of the bed, staring down contemptuously at Trevor. He spat his brother's name out in a violent whisper: "*Trevor!*" But Trevor remained lost to the world. Kerry suddenly hit Trevor sharply across the side of the face. "Trevor!" Trevor moaned in his sleep. Then he gripped hold of Trevor by the lapels of his jacket and shook him fiercely. "Come on! Wake up – *you!*" There came a snorting, choking noise from Trevor. He lifted his head in surprise, his eyes squinting open. Kerry let go and stood back, watching his brother coldly.

Trevor sat up on the bed, feeling his face and head, still only half awake. He groaned thickly. "W-what's . . . what's on?"

"It's me, Trev."

Trevor heard the voice, and peered up at the figure standing beside his bed. "W-what? . . . who's there? . . ."

"Kerry."

Trevor frowned, groping round his bedside table for the alarm clock. "What time is it?"

"Half seven," Kerry told him.

Trevor groaned, lifting his legs off the bed. He sat on the edge, holding his head in his hands. "My head! Feels like a ton of bricks come down on top . . ."

"Out drinking last night," said Kerry coldly. "Victory booze-up with your mates."

Trevor slowly looked up at Kerry. "What you doing here this time of the morning?"

"Things to tell you. Things to say."

"Won't it keep?" Trevor's voice was edged with suspicion.

"No," said Kerry bluntly. "I'm on my way to the police station."

"*Police? . . .*"

"Yeah. Make a statement to them."

Trevor was now fully awake. "What statement?"

"I know all about it, Trev," Kerry told him. "About Todd. And about *you.* The whole set up. Todd fixed it so that you were made captain."

Trevor got up slowly from the bed. "You're out of your mind!"

Kerry shook his head. "Todd paid Dad a visit last night, after the speedway meeting. They had quite a long natter. I've got big ears." Kerry watched his brother's face grow hard and angry. "And this morning," Kerry added, "I'm going to have a very big mouth!"

Trevor stared at him for a moment. "No, kid," he said quietly. "No, I don't think so."

"So what you going to do, Trev?" asked Kerry. "Pull the tongue out me head?"

Trevor said nothing. He poured himself a glass of water and sipped it. Kerry walked up to Trevor and spoke angrily: "*I* can't be bought off! Put me in hospital – yeah, get on with it! But there's no way you can shut *me* up!"

"I'm not going to do anything to you, kid," said Trevor. He turned away from Kerry, and walked casually across the room. "It's not going to be necessary."

A sudden, yawning fear stole through Kerry. He paused. Then he asked: "What do you mean by that?"

Trevor gave a pleased grin. "Go on, spill your full. Only I hope you remember to tell the police about our old man and his dubious past."

Silence. Kerry gaped at his brother. So he knew. So he actually *knew.* And Trevor was allowing Todd to do this to Dad. He could hardly believe it. "So Todd's told you," he said flatly.

"Not half!" Trevor's voice was heavy with sarcasm. "King Cinder! For years our old man's played the big *I-am* in this town, fooled everyone, when all the time he was just a fraud."

"Streuth!" spat Kerry. "Coming from you!"

"Lay off!" warned Trevor.

"How much is Todd paying you, Trev?"

"Todd's done a lot for me," Trevor told him, "more than the old man ever did."

"Todd's *using* you!"

"He's taking me where I want to go, kid. Into big-league speedway."

Kerry was still convinced that Trevor didn't fully understand what was going on. It was inconceivable that he would side with Todd. "Todd's got you on his payroll and he's using it to blackmail Dad!" Kerry explained. "That's why I came here . . ."

Trevor sighed wearily. "Look, kid, just go away."

"Todd was born in Barton. Him and Dad are old enemies."

"I know that," said Trevor.

"Then stop being a sucker!" Kerry shouted.

Trevor shook his head and spoke quietly: "I'm not being a sucker . . ."

"Todd aims to run a protection racket here in Barton. He's leaning heavily on Dad to get it started. Wants to get his own back on him."

"Yeah!" Trevor grinned at him. "Yeah, you're right. Clever kid!"

The blood drained out of Kerry's face. His worst fears had come true. "So you know everything about it?" he asked his brother in a sad, sick voice.

"Course I do," Trevor told him. "Todd explained it all."

"And you're letting Todd do this to Dad?"

Trevor nodded, smiling. "What do I owe the old man? Eh? *Nothing!* I owe Todd Edwards a lot. All I'm bothered about, is getting into big-league racing. It's that simple, kid."

A sudden fury surfaced in Kerry. "Streuth, *you!—*"

"Right!" snapped Trevor. "OK, I'm a bad lot. I get it from Dad!"

Kerry surged forward, his fist raised. His brother quickly side-stepped and gripped hold of Kerry tightly round the neck, half choking him. Trevor spoke quietly: "Now get out of here, kid, while you're still in one piece." Trevor released Kerry suddenly and pushed him towards the door. "Move yourself. And I mean today!"

Kerry leaned against the back of the door, panting heavily as he felt his neck. He looked across at Trevor. "You and Todd are going to fetch it!"

"Go on," said Trevor wearily, "get lost!"

"Don't leave town, will you, Trev? The police will want words with you!"

Trevor suddenly tensed up. He stared at Kerry. "You're not going to the police!"

"Just watch me!" spat Kerry.

"But the old man," said Trevor anxiously, "it'll all come out about him."

"If it's true about Dad—"

"It's true!"

"Then that's the way it goes." Kerry's voice was hard and determined. "He gets it as well!"

Trevor had grown tense, his face knotted with anxiety. "He'll be the one to suffer, don't you see?"

"I wouldn't bank on that," Kerry said. "Dad's got broad shoulders." Kerry swung open the door. He looked back gravely at his brother. "But *you* – you'll never get near that speedway stadium again!" Kerry moved out into the passageway.

Trevor stepped forward. "Look, don't go to the police—"

"See you in court, Trev!" Kerry pulled the door shut with a bang.

Trevor dashed over, and then stopped by the door, thinking hard. He listened to Kerry's footsteps pound down the passageway. He crossed over to the window and dragged back the curtains. After a moment, he saw Kerry run from the alleyway, and walk swiftly down the street, glancing back now and then to see if Trevor was coming after him. No way of catching him now, thought Trevor, too many people about. What would be the point, anyway? He couldn't keep Kerry silent for ever.

He had to get down to the canal. To tell Todd. And quick.

9 Home Truths

Kerry saw his father looking out of the living-room window as he crossed the back yard. He was waiting for Kerry in the kitchen. "Kerry! Where the devil have you been?" Kerry was silent. He tried to pass but his father blocked his path. "Hey? Your bed's not been slept in. I've been dead worried!"

Kerry looked at him impassively. "I was indoors last night when Todd Edwards came," Kerry said, watching his face. "I heard what was said between you. I heard everything." His father was silent, and now Kerry's voice was edged with aggression. "Well, go on," said Kerry, "tell me. Is it true? Did you get to the top the way Todd said?"

His father looked down at the palms of his hands. "Yes . . ." His voice seemed to come from deep inside him.

"Got your reputation with the help of double-dealers?" Kerry could hear his voice shaking.

There was a pause before his father replied. "What Todd said, it's all true . . ."

Kerry looked quickly away, as if his jaw had been punched. So there it was, out in the open at last. All of Kerry's doubts, suspicions, his worst fears, realised in a moment. He felt like throwing up. "And have you done what he told you?" asked Kerry, his head still turned away. "Contacted the other shopkeepers and people?"

"I made some phone calls last night."

Kerry glanced back at him. "Had no choice, did you?"

"Look," began his father, "I don't want to make excuses—"
Kerry's face hardened with contempt. "That would be pretty difficult!"

"I know what I did in the past was very wrong. Just . . . I'm just very ashamed . . ."

"Dead easy, ain't it? Sorry afterwards!"

"Kerry, try to understand," his father pleaded. "It was very tough, getting into the world championships. But I made it, all off my own bat, nobody helped me."

"Bully for you!" Kerry sneered.

"Look," said his father, "give me a chance. I'm doing my best to explain." Kerry fell silent and let his father continue: "Suddenly I was in a different league altogether – the international stakes. It was all new to me, another world. Full of big-timers with fat wallets and swanky talk. Sharks on the make. I was young and ambitious, I got taken in. Before I knew what was happening, it had all begun. The double-dealing and cheating, the bribes . . ."

"Sounds so innocent," said Kerry cynically, "like it was an accident or something!"

"I'm telling you how it happened," his father insisted. "Suddenly, there I was, involved with shady operators, crooks. Men like Todd Edwards."

"The way I see it, there's not a lot of difference between the two of you!" Kerry said savagely.

His father sat down and spoke wearily: "I got out of speedway before my time. Chucked it in when I realised what I'd become."

"And that makes everything OK, does it?"

"I have to live with it every single day."

"Don't make me laugh!" Kerry sneered. "You've lived off your legend for years! The restaurant's even named after it."

"Kerry, I had to earn a living somehow after your mother died, with you and Trevor to bring up—"

"Now don't come *that* one!" Kerry shouted hotly.

"I'm giving it to you straight!"

"A bit late in the day," Kerry snapped spitefully. "You let me grow up thinking you were somebody. I looked up to you, thought you were the greatest. Wanted to be like you. And *you* – you let me swallow it whole!"

"I . . . I just couldn't tell you, Kerry . . . couldn't bring myself to it."

"I went over to see Trevor early this morning," Kerry told him. "Tried to make him see that Todd was just using him to get back at you. You know what? I even threatened Trevor with the police – hoping it would scare him into breaking with Todd." Kerry stared bitterly at his father. "All so as to protect you. Because I couldn't *believe* it, what Todd said, thought there must be more to it – some reason why. I just couldn't believe that you were a crook."

There was a long silence. Finally, "What can I say?" asked his father.

"*Nothing!*" Kerry crossed to the passageway. "Nothing at all!" Kerry looked back at his father. "You and Todd and Trevor – you can all rot and the rest of Barton with you! I'm cutting free of this dung-heap!"

"Kerry! Kerry, no . . ."

"First train to London!"

Kerry went upstairs and swiftly packed a rucksack with clothes and a few personal belongings. He slung the rucksack over his shoulder, and then took a final look round the room. *His* room in the house he'd grown up in. He looked at the speedway posters covering the walls. Then he went out, slamming the door heavily behind him.

His father was waiting for him at the foot of the stairs. "Kerry, I know you're very upset—"

"Out of my way!" Kerry barged past him and went quickly across the hall.

"Kerry, please don't go!"

"Jump off!" He banged the back door in his father's face.

Trevor throttled down the canal track on his motorbike. As he approached Todd's barge, he saw that the red car had gone. For one terrible moment, he thought that Todd wasn't there, maybe pulled out, left Barton. Then he saw Todd moving about in the cabin. Trevor pulled up on the track beside the barge and blasted his horn three times. Todd peered out the cabin window.

"Todd!" shouted Trevor, as he waded out between the thick reeds towards the barge. Todd stepped out on to the deck, frowning.

Todd's eyes flicked over Trevor. "*What?*" he asked, in a clipped voice.

Trevor clambered on to the barge. "It's Kerry," he explained. "My kid brother. He knows everything! He's going to the police!"

Todd's face grew tense. Then, almost immediately, he regained his cool, self-assured composure. "Is he indeed?" he said quietly. He ushered Trevor into the cabin, and handed him a cup of hot, steaming coffee. "Drink that," he said, "and calm down."

The interior of the cabin was fairly spacious and luxurious. There were a couple of bunks, a kitchenette, some easy chairs, a dining-table, and a sideboard containing a cocktail cabinet.

Todd looked thoughtfully out of the cabin window. "He realises that going to the police will incriminate his father?"

Trevor sipped his coffee. "Kerry don't care. He's bent on telling the law everything!"

"And he went there immediately after calling on you?"

"Yeah!"

Todd was insistent. "You're *sure*?"

"I only know what he said," Trevor told him.

Todd remained calm. "All we can do now is bide our time until Clayton gets back."

"Where's he gone?"

Todd poured himself a cup of coffee. "He's gone into Barton. He's collecting the first protection instalments from the shopkeepers."

Trevor paced around, agitated and very tense. "Streuth! While Kerry spills his full to the law!"

"Cool down, Trevor." Todd waved dismissively. "Kerry made that threat in the heat of the moment. But actually going to the police station, sitting in an interview room and making a statement that will effectively ruin his father . . . " Todd shook his head and smiled. "I doubt if Kerry will go through with that."

"But what if he *has* done?"

Todd drank some coffee. "His statement will be pure supposition. Nothing can be proved, not a thing –" here Todd looked intently at Trevor – "Provided everyone stays calm and keeps their mouth shut. And then who will believe the story of a seventeen-year-old boy?"

Trevor sounded dubious. "I don't know . . . if the police start nosing around . . ."

"Then we deny everything," said Todd. "And if the going gets really hot, we simply disappear. *Caput!*"

"Maybe we should pull out now while the going's good," Trevor suggested.

Todd grew angry. "*No.* Only as a very last resort. I haven't come back to Barton, established this elaborate set-up, simply to back down because of master Kerry!"

"Kerry can cause a lot of trouble when he wants to," Trevor said tensely. "He's a pretty wild kid."

Todd bit into a digestive biscuit. "If your brother has really gone to the police, we'll soon know about it. But if it amounts to no more than an idle threat, then I think we should teach young Kerry a lesson or two . . ."

"How d'you mean?"

"We'll pick him up and bring him back here." Todd smiled.

"Have a quiet word."

"But we don't know for certain where he is!"

Todd thought for a moment. "Has he got a girlfriend?"

"Yeah," said Trevor. "Young Nikki . . ."

"When do they usually see each other?" Todd asked.

"Every day. They go to the same school."

"Right, this afternoon," Todd said. "Clayton will be back, and we'll know by then if there are any problems with the police." Todd poured himself a second cup of coffee and lit a cigar. "We'll snatch the girl when she leaves school. That'll bring Kerry to us. If Kerry's there with her, even better . . ."

Kerry had parked his motorbike in the cycle shed. The playground resounded with the noise of teeming, excited kids. It was the mid-morning break. Kerry weaved his way through the milling school children. Nikki was standing among a group of girls, classmates of hers. They were all giggling merrily over a joke.

Kerry came up and tapped Nikki on the shoulder. She had already spotted him crossing the playground. She gave him a cool glance. "Oh," she said, "so you're still alive."

"I couldn't pick you up for school this morning," Kerry said apologetically.

"Yeah, so I gathered!" Nikki nodded at Kerry's rucksack. "Going for a picnic?" she asked wryly.

"Want to have a chat . . ."

Nikki spoke tartly. "About *what?*"

"In private," Kerry insisted.

"There's nothing to talk about, so far as I'm concerned," Nikki said unpleasantly.

"*Please* . . ." Kerry moved away from the other girls and Nikki reluctantly followed.

"Come on, then. Let's have it," said Nikki sharply. Kerry was silent. He was unable to meet Nikki's gaze. "What do you want to chat about?" asked Nikki irritably.

"Sorry I was acting weird last night," Kerry mumbled.

"S'all right," said Nikki flippantly. "Get used to anything given time!" Kerry couldn't speak. "Well?" asked Nikki. "That all you wanted to say?"

"No," said Kerry quietly. "That's not all . . ."

And then, quietly, Kerry began to tell her everything.

Nulty watched the red car nose slowly through the market square. The fat, frog-faced one, whom Kerry said was called Clayton, drove alone. Nulty stood behind his stall and continued serving his customers, keeping his eyes fixed on the car.

Clayton parked the car fifty yards away along the kerb. He crossed the pavement over to a row of shops which stood behind the market. He went into a greengrocer's shop and spoke briefly to the proprietor, Stan Rogers, a man Nulty had known well for years. Stan looked Clayton up and down with a disgruntled air, as if the fat man was bad news. Then the proprietor went to the back of his shop, returning a moment later with a long sealed envelope. Stan handed the envelope to Clayton, who accepted it with a broad grin. Clayton stepped out of the shop, tucking the envelope into his inside jacket pocket.

Nulty called over to him. "Morning, sir!"

Clayton glanced round and grinned at Nulty. He walked over. "Wotchyer there, soldier!" he beamed. "How you doing?"

Nulty nodded sagely. "Aye sir, fine. How about y'self?"

"Wonder if you could help me, soldier," Clayton asked. "Got any idea where the *Jolly Sailor* pub is around here?"

Nulty smiled. "The *Jolly Sailor?* I know it well, sir! Oh, aye. I have a jar there m'self, very often, of a lunchtime."

Clayton looked pleased. "Oh, might see you in there today then, soldier. I've got a few more calls to make, then the pub for lunch." He smiled at Nulty. "Have a pint on me!" That would make up for tricking the old codger the other day.

"That'll be nice," said Nulty quietly. He explained to Clayton how to find the pub. Clayton thanked Nulty, walked back to the car and drove off.

When the vehicle was out of sight, Nulty grabbed his walking stick and limped over to the greengrocer's shop. "Hello there, Stan," grinned Nulty. "How's business?"

They were both quiet for a time after Kerry had finished explaining everything. He and Nikki were sitting on a low brick wall near the sportsfield. The playground was deserted. Lessons had resumed.

Nikki glanced at him. "Sounds like something out of a film."

"Yeah, I know . . ." said Kerry, still looking away from her.

"Certain you didn't dream it up?" Nikki asked lightly.

But Kerry wasn't in the mood. "Right wish I had done!"

"Can hardly believe it. All this going on in sleepy old

Barton!" Nikki bit into a Mars bar. "Want some?" Kerry shook his head.

"S'why I've been in such a mood, trying to fathom it all out," Kerry explained.

"Thought you were just green over Trevor getting made captain . . ."

Kerry shook his head. "I knew how it'd been swung for him."

"Never liked your brother," said Nikki pertly. "Thinks he's the greatest thing invented since sliced bread!"

"He's just a pawn in it anyway."

There was a pause. "So, what happens now?" asked Nikki.

Kerry glanced at her. "I told you! I'm catching the train to London."

"Goodbye, then!" Nikki said with sudden briskness.

Kerry stared at her. "I'm serious about it. Wanted to see you first. Say goodbye . . ."

"Right, well you've done that. Now you'd better shoot off." She looked across at him. "Go on, hop it! Catch that train!"

"I'm not joking, you know," said Kerry earnestly.

"Don't talk stupid!" Nikki scoffed. "You're not going to London!"

Kerry jumped down from the brick wall, picked up his rucksack and slung it over his shoulder. "Just watch me!" he said. But he didn't move. He just stood there, looking a bit embarrassed.

Nikki nodded. "The station's just down the road."

"Oh, drop the smart-alec bit!" said Kerry angrily.

Nikki answered fiercely: "If you stop talking soft!"

"*Who's* talking soft?"

"What you scuttling off to London for?"

"I'm not *scuttling* anywhere," he replied indignantly. "I'm splitting, that's what – getting out of Barton for good."

"Over your Dad?"

"Yeah!"

" 'Cause of the skeletons you found in his cupboard?"

Kerry sat down on the wall beside Nikki. He spoke pensively. "You think you know somebody, your own father, and then it turns out that through all these years you never knew him at all, he was someone different . . ."

"You never done nothing you're ashamed of?" Nikki asked.

Kerry looked at her. "Course I have – titchy things."

Nikki shrugged. "Well, there you go."

"Come on!" said Kerry angrily. "That's different – no comparison!"

Nikki wouldn't be put down. "Just goes to show," she said, "nobody's perfect." Nikki grinned impishly. "Show me somebody's perfect – go on! – and *I'll* keep well clear of them!"

"My old man made out he was somebody," Kerry said lumpishly.

"No he never – *you* did. Your Dad's never come the great *I-am* over speedway," said Nikki. Kerry remained silent. "But then *you* built him up, I've heard you talk! Then suddenly you find out he's got a few pockmarks like most people and you can't take it!"

Kerry swallowed this. "He could've come clean," was all he could say.

Nikki lectured him fiercely: "So what was he meant to do? Sit down at breakfast one morning over the boiled eggs and toast and say, *Hey son, there's something I've got to tell you . . .* Come on!"

Kerry shook his head. "You still don't get it," he told her. "Dad was someone I really – I dunno, I really looked up to . . ."

Nikki groaned wearily. She looked at Kerry. Suddenly she said: "You're a great big baby! Hero worship – that's for kids. You got to take people as they come! What's the matter with you?" Nikki asked. "OK, your old man did wrong – at least he *knows* it was crooked. Now he's paying for it and he needs your help!"

"He hasn't asked for my help . . ."

"Course he hasn't *asked*, you daft 'aporth!" Nikki could have willingly thumped him one. "But who else has he got, except you? And now you're getting off out of it because you can't stand the smell of dirty knickers!"

Kerry stood up angrily. "Jump off!"

Nikki got up and stood face to face with Kerry, her hands

sitting firmly on her hips. She had a real go at him. "It's all about *you*, ain't it? Poor little you! The story of your sad life! How do you think your Dad feels? He's not having a ball exactly!" Kerry turned away. For a moment, Nikki thought she'd blown it. But Kerry didn't move off. He stood there red-faced and silent. Nikki went up to him. She spoke quietly: "Your Dad brought you up with a shirt on your back. Now he's in bad trouble and he needs you around, right?"

Nikki was right. Of course she was right! Kerry had known the truth of what she said all along really. He just needed someone to say it. "Yeah," he muttered, almost to himself. There was a pause. Then Kerry looked up and grinned. "I've missed it anyway," he said.

"Missed what?"

"The train to London."

Nikki laughed. She punched him lightly in the stomach. "Then what are you going on about?" She began to stroll across the tarmac towards the school buildings. She glanced back at Kerry. "Coming into class, then?"

Kerry shook his head. "I'm going truant for the day. See what I can do to help Dad."

"Can't I help out?"

"No," said Kerry, "ta all the same, Nikki."

"See you tonight, then?"

Kerry wasn't certain. "Yeah, maybe." He frowned. "Depends on what happens..."

Nikki waved to him as she crossed the vacant playground. Kerry stood there and watched her until she disappeared into the classroom block.

Kerry knew he had to move fast. He had wasted a lot of time throwing his moody, and he suspected that Todd or his side-kick would have begun their collection of protection money from the shops in town. Once that was under way, Kerry feared it would be difficult to rid Barton of Todd Edwards without damaging Dad in the process. He would check with Nulty first, to see if he knew anything. Then take a quiet look down by the canal...

As he sped through the town, Kerry felt as if a great weight had been lifted from his shoulders. He still had to make his peace with his father, but he wasn't ready to do that just yet. It would take time to find the courage to go back and admit he was wrong.

Kerry pulled up beside Nulty's fish-stall. "OK then, Nulty?" he asked the old man.

"Aye, aye!" Nulty waved dismissively. He was excited about something. "Listen, lad, I've found out something for you. Todd's mate, he's been out and about today collecting money." Kerry's heart sunk. Nulty continued: "And it's all in aid of a protection racket. Know the sort of set-up I mean, lad?"

"Yeah, Nulty, I know . . ."

"That must be Todd's game here in Barton," Nulty suggested.

"Have people been paying up?" asked Kerry.

"The one or two I saw – aye, they paid."

"*Sure*, Nulty?"

Nulty pointed across to the shops behind them. "The fella that owns the greengrocers over there, Stan Rogers. And I chatted up the publican of the *Jolly Sailor* at lunchtime. They both handed over a hundred pounds."

Kerry sat there on his motorbike for a moment, deep in thought. "Any help to you, lad?" asked Nulty.

Kerry swung his bike away from the kerb. "Yeah," he said, "thanks a lot, Nulty . . ."

Afternoon sunlight dazzled the surface of the canal. Water lilies floated lazily. The scent of honeysuckle drifted through the trees. Bumble bees droned heavily around the cow-parsley which fringed the canal track. There was the drone of a tractor on a distant hill.

Kerry frowned. The barge lay deserted. The red car had gone. Kerry sat on his motorbike between the trees and pondered. He would wait here awhile to see if Todd and Clayton reappeared.

10 Snatch

Just before four o'clock the red Maxi pulled up by the kerb opposite the main gates of Fletcher Street Comprehensive. In a few minutes the school grounds were thronged as boys and girls noisily made their way out.

"Hey," said Trevor, pointing, "that's Nikki over there!" She was walking with a group of schoolmates out through the main gates of the school. Trevor frowned. "No sign of Kerry, though . . ."

"Which one is Nikki?" Todd asked.

Trevor singled her out with his finger. "With that crowd of girls passing the post box. She's wearing the blue dress and white jacket. With the long brown hair."

Todd fired the starter. "Right," he said, "we'll pick the girl up." He kept the engine running, waiting for Trevor to get out of the car before they moved forward.

"What will you do to her?" Trevor asked uneasily. "I mean, you won't harm her, will you?"

"Get going now, Trevor," Clayton told him.

"But what's going to happen to Nikki?" persisted Trevor.

Todd spoke quietly: "Trevor. Be missing . . ."

Trevor clambered out of the car, slamming the rear door. He watched it pull away from the kerb and weave its way across to the opposite side of the street. Nikki, walking with her schoolmates, was a hundred yards down the pavement. Trevor watched helplessly as the car crept slowly up on her.

Clayton pulled on a pair of black leather gloves as he watched through the windscreen. He ran his tongue over his lips.

"We'll take her when she's alone," Todd said.

At the end of the street, Nikki left the group of girls, taking the road towards the Kitchener estate. She waved to her schoolmates and called out: "See you tomorrow, then!"

Todd watched. "Good," he said. He swung the car down a side road.

Clayton frowned. "Where are you going?" he asked.

"Short cut," Todd told him. "We'll intercept her."

Nikki walked down the pavement of the quiet, tree-lined road, humming to herself. She was deep in thought. She was glad that things were all right again between Kerry and her. She wondered anxiously about the situation with his father and the men who were trying to blackmail him. She still couldn't credit that such a thing had happened to Mr Hutson. Surely it would be simpler to call in the police! But, she shrugged to herself, it would all sort itself out. Most things did . . .

As she passed under the shadow of a tree she heard a metallic click and the whine of a door and looked up. Violent red flashed before her eyes. She saw a car door swing open across the pavement in front of her. A tall man climbed out, smiling at Nikki. Oh no, not another of them! Push off, thought Nikki, find somebody your own age.

"Hello, Nikki . . ." said the man.

Nikki gasped. He knows my name! Then she realised. There before her was the man Kerry had described. There was Todd.

Nikki opened her mouth to scream. Suddenly a big black hand closed in over her face.

Kerry peered in through the living-room window. He saw his father sitting in the armchair, bent over, elbows across his thighs, brooding. He stared at the array of prize-cups lining the bookcase in the corner.

Kerry stepped tentatively across the hall. He braced

himself, opened the living-room door and stepped inside.

"Hello, Dad . . ." Kerry said.

A couple of minutes later, his father was pouring out two small glasses of sherry. He handed one to Kerry. "The whole thing was my fault," he said, "letting you find out that way. I should've come clean, told you about it."

Kerry shook his head. "How could you, Dad? Something like that . . . ?"

"You were bound to find out sooner or later."

"Maybe so," admitted Kerry. "But I acted stupid this morning."

"You were justified."

Kerry looked at him. "No, I wasn't. Sorry for what I said."

His father patted Kerry's arm. "Well, I'm glad you're back."

They silently raised their glasses and sipped the sherry. After a moment, Kerry said: "I found out from Nulty that the protection ring has started operating. Clayton's been in Barton today, collecting the money."

"If only I could *do* something! I feel useless," complained his father. "Todd's got me exactly where he wants me."

"But the protection racket could be a way of putting a stop to Todd," Kerry suggested.

"How d'you mean?"

Kerry explained: "Well, I reckon if too many people got wind of the protection racket, what with the risk, Todd would just cut his losses and clear out."

His father looked doubtful. "Todd's not going to advertise the fact that he's running a protection racket."

"No, but what if *we* quietly put the word about?" suggested Kerry enthusiastically. "An anonymous phone call to the police saying that a certain member of the London underworld is here, in Barton." Kerry watched his father's face for a reaction. "Make things too sticky for Todd to operate."

"Maybe it's better simply to go to the police and tell them the whole story!"

"And drop yourself in it?" protested Kerry. "You'd never

be able to show your face in Barton again."

"I'd get what I deserve."

Kerry went up to his father and punched him lightly on the shoulder. "Stop feeling sorry for yourself, Dad!" he said. "We've got to work a way out of this. Fix Todd without letting ourselves in for it."

"Todd's pretty shrewd. The police have never caught him out yet, what chance do *we* stand?"

Kerry sipped his sherry, pulled a face and plonked the glass down on the sideboard. "If everyone co-operates and pays Todd, what does he do next?"

"What're you getting at?"

Kerry paced up and down. "Todd will soon get fed up sitting on his barge gathering in protection money . . ."

"He'll put the price up, then. Start squeezing harder. He wants to bleed this town dry."

"But will the shopkeepers keep paying up?" asked Kerry.

"Todd will just put more pressure on me to persuade them," his father assured him.

The phone began ringing. His father stepped into the hall and lifted the receiver.

Kerry leant against the edge of the table. He frowned. Somehow he had to find a way to spur his father out of his defeatism. They were getting nowhere fast like this . . .

"Kerry, it's for you . . ." Kerry went into the hall. It's Nikki," his father told him. "She's in a phone box."

Kerry spoke cheerfully into the receiver: "Wotchyer there!"

But he didn't recognise the voice as Nikki's. He heard a panic-riddled scream. "*Kerry!—*" It almost broke his eardrum.

Kerry froze. "Nikki! . . . *what?*" He listened. There was silence on the line. "*Nikki!*" Kerry shouted into the receiver. Then he heard the voice. Todd's voice. Cool and disdainful. "Hello, Kerry. My name's Todd Edwards. I don't believe we've met."

"What have you done with her?" Kerry managed to say.

"If you want your girlfriend back safe and sound," breathed the voice, "then I suggest you come out to my barge and collect her . . ." The receiver was replaced. There came the drone of the open line.

Kerry banged down the receiver. His father was there beside him. "What's *up?*"

Kerry dashed across the hall, down the passageway, out the back of the house. He shouted back: "*Todd!* He's got Nikki!"

Kerry tore through the heavy rush-hour traffic, dangerously cutting between vehicles, ignoring the amber beacon of traffic lights. His body strained forward over the bike, urging it to move faster. He gripped the handlebars, his eyes rigidly fixed on the road ahead. If anything happened to Nikki, vowed Kerry, then he personally would pay for Todd's funeral.

He wove down the woodland path, moving the bike slowly, keeping its engine as quiet as possible. He reached the edge of the woodlands, where the canal track cut through, dismounted and leant the bike up against a thick tree trunk, concealing the machine from view. Kerry looked around. He had come to this very spot only a few hours before. Yet it seemed like an age. He crept forward between the ferns and peered out at the barge. He could see Todd and Clayton sitting in the cabin, talking. The red car stood at the side of the track. There was no sign of Nikki.

Keeping his eyes on the barge, Kerry quickly pulled off his boots and socks. Then he removed his jacket, bundled the boots and clothes up together, and hid them among the ferns. He crawled out to the verge of the canal track. Choosing his moment, he raced quickly across the track, crouched double, running like an elk. He reached the canal bank and slid down it, then paused for a moment to catch his breath.

He looked towards the cabin. Todd and Clayton were still inside, in the midst of an intense discussion. Kerry peered round the side of the barge, taking a close look at its rear. Then he silently crawled through the reeds, right down to the water's edge. He lowered himself into the water, shivering at the sudden cold, and crouched down in the water until it swelled up to his throat. Gradually, quietly, Kerry waded out towards the far side of the barge.

He was nearing the rear of the barge. There was a *swack*

as the cabin door slid open. Footsteps on the deck. Panic sunk through Kerry. His face twisted round. He saw Todd stepping across the deck, followed by Clayton. Kerry gulped down a lungful of air and quickly plunged his head into the muddy water, his body totally disappearing beneath the surface. He made a small splash as he went under.

Todd heard the splash. He paused there on the deck, listening intently, frowning. Then he crossed to the side of the barge. Small ripples moved out across the muddy surface beneath the barge. Todd stood there for a moment, his eyes raking across the canal, the track and the edge of the woodlands. "See you later," he said to Clayton.

"OK," said Clayton, going back into the cabin. Todd clambered off the barge and walked over to the car.

There was a plop and Kerry's head appeared above the water, coated thickly with mud. He gasped for air, wiping the filth out of his eyes. He heard a car engine start up nearby. Kerry glanced towards the track and watched the car move off into the distance.

Kerry waded forward through the water. Guiding himself with his hands he edged round the vessel. He saw Clayton sitting in the cabin reading a newspaper.

Gingerly Kerry hauled himself up on the side of the barge and tentatively peered in through the window of the rear cabin. Nikki lay stretched out on the bottom bunk. Her wrists were tied together behind her back and her ankles were bound. A large patch of sticking plaster covered her mouth. She lay on her side with her back to the window.

Kerry tapped against the window with his knuckle.

No reaction from Nikki. She lay quite still.

Kerry tapped again, louder this time. Nikki twisted round, glancing up at the window. She saw Kerry and sat up.

Nikki swung her legs off the bunk and stood unsteadily. Kerry pointed to the bolt which secured the cabin door on the inside. Nikki nodded her head. She eased herself down until she stood on the floor. Then she shuffled unsteadily, almost over-balancing, across the cabin floor until she reached the door. She twisted round, her hands searching desperately for the bolt. She gripped hold of it and wrenched it backwards.

Kerry had scrambled on to the deck and now came into the cabin. They stood by the door, listening tensely, but there was no sound from the other cabin.

"Let's get this off!" Kerry whispered. He ripped the sticking plaster off Nikki's face, tearing it quickly from her lips.

"*Ouch!*"

Kerry put a finger to his lips. "*Shssh!*"

Nikki felt her mouth. Kerry looked at her. "You all right?"

"Yeah, fantastic! How are you?" she whispered back.

"I'll get you untied."

"Ta!"

Nikki twisted round and presented her bound wrists to Kerry. He stooped and began untying the rope, using his teeth to budge the heavy knots. "Todd drove off just now," he whispered.

"I know. Overheard them talking in here just now."

"Todd say where he was going?" asked Kerry. He knelt down and began untying her ankles, again using his teeth to loosen the knots.

"Into Barton," whispered Nikki as she massaged her wrists. "Collect some protection money . . ."

Kerry unwound the rope from Nikki's ankles. He straightened up. "*Quick!*"

They both moved furtively on to the deck. Kerry climbed out and stood in the water, then Nikki lowered herself on to his back. Kerry waded out around the outside of the barge towards the bank. They crouched over the slime, through the reeds and up the side of the bank. "*Now!*" whispered Kerry.

They ran for it. Crouched double, not daring to look back, they raced across the track and crawled quickly between the ferns on the far side.

Kerry sat on the ground, quickly pulling on his boots. Nikki gripped the motorbike handlebars and pushed the machine awkwardly over to the woodland path. They both kept a wary eye on the barge, but there was no sound to be heard from it.

"Todd's gone and landed himself in it this time," said Kerry, keeping his voice low. "Nabbing you is his first bad move."

Nikki glanced at him wryly. "Glad to have been of use!"

"Now we can really fix him."

"How d'you mean?"

Kerry said: "I've got an idea . . . if my plan works, then we'll be rid of Todd for good!"

"*What* plan?"

Kerry got to his feet, pulling on his jacket. "Let's get away from here first!"

Kerry mounted his motorbike and kicked it violently into action. He glanced back at Nikki. "Come on!" She climbed on the pillion and clung hold of Kerry.

Kerry revved and the motorbike wound away along the woodland path, quickly becoming just a murmur of sound as it disappeared between the trees.

As Todd drove back along the canal track towards the barge he suddenly saw Clayton standing on the track, waving his arms urgently. He pulled up beside him, got out and slammed the door. "*What?*"

Clayton spoke nervously: "The girl – she's got free."

Todd struck him across the jaw. "How did it happen?"

"The door was open," Clayton said miserably. Todd's eyes angrily scanned the surrounding woodlands. Clayton added apologetically: "I didn't know a thing about it."

Todd chewed the name like a cashew-nut. "Kerry . . ."

Richard Hutson watched Nikki anxiously. She was curled up in one of the living-room armchairs, a blanket wrapped round her, sipping a bowl of soup. "Nikki," he said, "I'll phone your parents."

Nikki glanced up. "No, don't go and tell them about it, they'd have a fit! We're not on the phone at home anyway . . ."

Kerry had changed his clothes, and stepped into the room, pulling on his jacket. His father turned to him. "I'm going to phone the police," he said.

"No, Dad—"

"It's time something was done about Todd Edwards!"

"If you go to the police, you know what'll happen," Kerry said. "Todd will start slinging mud."

"Let him! This has gone far enough! I'm not prepared to stand by while you kids get menaced and assaulted—"

"Listen to me, Dad—"

"Just because my reputation might be put at risk!"

Kerry said: "I'd thought of taking Nikki to the police station and getting her to make a complaint against Todd . . ."

"It must be reported!" insisted his father.

"And then letting on to Todd that the police are involved," Kerry continued. "Scare him into clearing out of Barton."

Nikki put down her bowl of soup. "But the police might get to Todd and question him before he's had time to scarper," she said.

"Right," agreed Kerry. "But what if Todd thinks you really *have* gone to the police, when all the time you're sitting at home here?"

"How's that?" Nikki asked.

Kerry explained: "There's no way Todd can check out whether you've reported it or not, short of walking into the police station!" Kerry looked at Dad. "More likely he'll pull out of town quick – then we'll be free of Todd. And there won't be any coppers sniffing round asking awkward questions."

His father wasn't convinced. "But why should Todd believe that Nikki's bringing charges against him?"

"Trevor," said Kerry. "I'll tell *him* that Nikki's dropping him in it together with Todd and Clayton. Then Trevor will go running to Todd."

"Trevor might skip out of town, leave Todd to his own devices," said Nikki.

"In that case I'll go and tell Todd myself," Kerry said.

"What if he calls your bluff?" asked Nikki.

Kerry shrugged. "Then we're back to square one. But at least it's worth a try!"

"No, Kerry. I want Todd reckoned with. I'm going to call the police right now!" said his father.

"Wait, Dad." Kerry went up to him. "Give me this one chance. See how it turns out! We've got nothing to lose."

But his father needed persuading. "Todd won't fall for it," he said. "He'll never believe that we've gone to the police."

Kerry glanced down at Nikki. "But it's different if Todd thinks Nikki and her parents are making the complaint. They're outside the family, Todd's got no hold over them."

There was a long pause. A bluebottle buzzed against the window pane. Eventually, Kerry's father slowly nodded his head. "All right," he said. "But leave Trevor out of it."

"No, Dad," Kerry said firmly, "Trevor's got to be scared off as well. Otherwise with Todd gone he'll more than likely use what he knows to blackmail you in exactly the same way."

"Trevor would never do that! He's only mixed up in this because of Todd's smooth talk."

"Sorry, Dad," Kerry said gently. "Trevor sold you out. He helped Todd plot to kidnap Nikki." He paused before adding: "Trevor will do anything to get what he wants."

His father moved pensively to the fireplace. "I don't know, Trevor! Trevor . . ."

"Nobody forced him to get mixed up with Todd," Kerry said. "He brought it all on himself."

"I know! But I can't just write him off like that . . ."

There was a pause. Kerry said: "I dunno, Dad, but maybe he'll see things differently when this is over and forgotten. Maybe it'll straighten him out."

"It all feels like my failure."

Kerry looked at his father. "I'd better get moving," he said grimly. Kerry got up to leave and Nikki followed. Outside, Nikki watched tensely as he strapped on his helmet. "Todd might turn dangerous," she said after a moment.

"Yeah, or else throw in the towel and clear off quick. That's what I'm counting on."

Nikki pecked Kerry lightly on the cheek. "Watch your step," she whispered.

"I'll be OK," he said. He pushed down his visor. "Things have got to happen fast. Todd won't swallow it if time drags on and it's obvious that the police aren't coming. It's all got to take him by surprise." He sounded frightened. "Wish me luck."

"Luck," she said. And stood there a long time after he had turned out of the back lane, hugging her arms around her body.

11 On the Track

Kerry spotted his brother as he rode across the sportsground towards the practice track. Trevor was sitting on the cropped grass next to Tom, smoking a cigarette, watching two members of his team race it out on the track. Groups of riders stood around watching the contest, or chatting idly among themselves.

Kerry parked his bike a good distance away, dumped his helmet, and walked on. Tom glanced round and spotted Kerry. "Hey, Trev – here's your kid brother!" Trevor looked round sharply. Tom grinned. "He's a keen one, ain't he?"

Trevor watched Kerry uneasily, stubbing his cigarette out on the grass. He looked abruptly away. Tom put up his hand as Kerry came up to them. "Wotchyer there, Kerry!" he beamed.

Kerry ignored him and stood over his brother, hands on his hips, staring down at Trevor. "Hello there, *Captain,*" he said sarcastically.

Trevor kept his eyes on the track.

Tom frowned. "What's up then, Kerry?"

"Better ask the Captain here."

Trevor spoke thinly. "Clear off, Kerry. Do it now," he advised.

Kerry didn't move. "They got Nikki, Trev. Just thought you'd like to know. They picked her up and took her to the barge."

"I'm warning you!" snapped Trevor, his eyes still on the race.

Tom stared at the two brothers, wondering what was up between them.

Kerry continued: "Only it didn't quite work out as planned. 'Cause I've just been out there and got her free. And right now Nikki's sitting in Barton police station making a full statement." Trevor suddenly looked up at Kerry. "And she's naming Todd Edwards as responsible," Kerry added, with perfect timing.

Trevor stared at Kerry for a long moment. Tom was watching. "What's he on about, Trev?" Tom asked.

Trevor's voice was tight and fierce. "Some madcap idea Kerry's got hold of!" He stood up and walked away from Kerry. "Why don't you leave off, eh?"

Kerry followed him. "Thought I'd better warn you," he told his brother, "so you can get your story right for when the police start asking questions."

Trevor swung round. "*What* questions?"

"It's all going in Nikki's statement," Kerry said. "About how Todd fixed it to get you made captain."

Trevor looked as if he had been punched in the gut. The blood suddenly drained from his face. Tom stared at Kerry. "That's not funny, Kerry."

Kerry kept watching Trevor. "You're dead right, Tom. Not funny at all. Just happens to be true."

Trevor tried to chuck it off. "Take no notice of him, Tom," he advised. He looked at Kerry. "Can't stand the thought of it, can you?" Trevor sneered. "Your brother riding as team-captain? Your brother instead of *you?*"

"Smart thinking, Trev," Kerry acknowledged. "Only you're going to need a bit more than that for the police!"

Trevor was suddenly seized with anger. He began to approach Kerry slowly, his eyes full of menace. "You've just made a lot of trouble for yourself, kid."

"Maybe I have."

"I'm going to beat hell out of you!"

"Clobbering me can't help you now," Kerry said flatly.

The practice race had finished. The two riders roared onto

the perimeter of the track. Tom glanced round at them.

"Time you were taught a few lessons!" Trevor shouted.

"Trev," said Tom flatly. "It's our turn for racing." It was a good chance to break this up. "Come on. Quick little spin round the track, get rid of those cobwebs."

But Trevor was looking at Kerry. "There's a little matter here that needs sorting first."

A number of the riders had gathered in a circle around Trevor and Kerry, their curiosity aroused by the chance of watching a fight. Others were strolling up and joining the audience. Kerry glanced at the riders. "Whose benefit is this for, Trev?" Kerry asked.

"Yours alone, kid," he was told.

"Aiming to convince Tom and the others that you're still straight?"

Trevor grabbed hold of Kerry by the lapels of his jacket and swung him sideways so violently that he went tumbling to the ground. He leaned right over Kerry, his face pinched and hard, taut with anger. Kerry twisted away from him, rolling across the grass, but Trevor caught hold of Kerry by the scruff of his neck and dragged him up. "Now!" he shouted. "Let's hear you take that back!"

"Jump off!" yelled Kerry.

Tom stepped forward and placed his hand firmly on Trevor's shoulder. "Let go of him, Trev," he told the team-captain.

Trevor glanced round. "You *what*?"

"Leave him alone."

Kerry pulled himself free of Trevor and moved away, wiping his fist across his mouth.

Trevor turned on Tom. "What you doing?" he wanted to know. "What's on?"

"He's just a kid," said Tom. "No match for you."

"You heard what he said!"

"Kerry must have a reason," Tom said quietly. "He's not going to risk getting his head knocked off for nothing."

Trevor shouted: "That kid's green with envy right up to his back teeth!"

Tom remained calm. "He's never acted like it before.

Kerry's always turned up in all weathers to support us."

Trevor sank back. He stared at Tom for a long moment. He looked across at his team of riders gathered round. They all watched Trevor impassively. "Look," he breathed, "you don't believe *him?*"

Tom said: "Everyone wondered why Campbell retired so sudden."

"He was paid off to make way for Trevor," Kerry put in.

Trevor jabbed his fist angrily at Kerry. "Shut your *face!*"

Kerry came back hard. "Better get out of Barton quick, Trev, before the law comes calling!"

Trevor made for Kerry. Tom stepped forward, blocking his path. "Leave it, Kerry!" he warned, staring hard at Trevor.

Trevor glared at Tom. "What you siding with him for?" he demanded.

There was a pause. Tom spoke with a tinge of regret in his voice: "We'll all be pretty glad to find out, Trev, that you're straight."

Trevor stared at him in disbelief. He stood there, completely stunned. He watched Kerry turn slowly away and walk off, back towards his motorbike. Trevor shouted after his brother: "Just you wait, kid – I'll *do* you!"

Kerry stopped to shout back at Trevor. "You know something, Trev – the trouble is you don't even know what you've done is wrong!"

Trevor looked at Tom. "What is this, Tom?" His voice shook.

"You tell us," came the reply.

"The kid's a liar!"

"Then you've got no worries."

Trevor caught something in Tom's tone. "How d'you mean? What you going to do?"

"Ask a few questions," said Tom.

"Questions?"

"Yeah, that's right, Trev," said Tom. "Have a chat with our ex-Captain Campbell for starters. Then find out if this bloke Todd really exists." Trevor wiped his hand down across his face. "Stay away from here for a bit, mate. Stay away until this business is sorted out." And Tom walked away. The other riders followed him, turning their backs on Trevor, and crossing over to their motorbikes parked at the side of the track.

Trevor stood there, a solitary figure. He shouted hopelessly after his team-members: "That kid's got you hooked on a pack of lies!"

Nobody was listening.

As Kerry rode away from the sportsground, he watched his own reflection in the driving mirror. He stared intently down at it as if the face he saw there was a stranger to him.

"Well come on then!" shouted Trevor, angrily. "You're the man with all the big ideas!"

"Get yourself a drink, Trevor," Todd told him.

"No thanks!"

Todd turned and looked at Trevor across the interior of the barge cabin. "Then calm down!"

Trevor turned to Clayton, who stood beside him near the sideboard. "D'you hear him?" he asked the fat man. Clayton was silent. Trevor glared at Todd. "*Calm down,* he says! Fantastic! With that bird Nikki in Barton police station telling the law everything!"

"If we lose our nerve now," Todd said, "then we're finished."

Trevor sat down. "I'm finished in this town anyway. I'll never ride for *The Barons* again, thanks to Kerry shouting off his mouth."

"You over-reacted. Kerry offered nothing but hearsay."

"Until certain questions get answered," replied Trevor.

"He's right, Todd," Clayton chimed in. "Too many people are wise to us. Let's cut our losses."

Todd gave Clayton a quick, angry glance. "We wouldn't be in this situation but for you!"

"Now come on!" Clayton protested.

"Unable to guard a teenage girl efficiently!"

"We underestimated Kerry," said Clayton quietly. "He's brought all this on us . . ."

Todd paced to the window and looked out across the canal water. "Well now we're going to deal with that kid once and for all."

"Bit late in the day," commented Trevor.

Todd said: "We pick up Kerry. We hold him here. Then," Todd pointed at Trevor, "we get *your* father to paper over the cracks with the police."

"What about Nikki's statement?" asked Trevor.

"A kid's prank," said Todd blandly. "All a simple misunderstanding." Todd smiled. "We shall be glad to accept her apologies."

Trevor shook his head. "The law are bound to question Kerry."

"Right," agreed Todd, "but when your father has been to the police and explained that it was all merely a practical joke, Kerry won't contradict it."

"He'll tell the truth more likely!" Trevor said.

"And just look stupid? You keep forgetting," insisted Todd, "nothing can be *proved*."

It had become clear that Todd was just clutching at straws. "They'll prove it," Trevor remarked dryly, "if they try hard enough."

Clayton said anxiously: "Once the police find out who we are, Todd, that's *it!*"

"And how are we going to grab Kerry anyway?" Trevor wanted to know. "We don't even know where he is!"

Todd looked at them. They were ganging up on him, he was gradually losing control. He crossed over to the sideboard and poured himself a stiff drink. Todd sipped it slowly, playing for time. Then he lit a cigar. He had to give himself time to think.

When Todd spoke again, he was calm but adamant. "I'm not going to get beaten by some pimply faced schoolkid!"

Trevor shook his head. "It's no good, Todd. I've had enough."

Todd spoke earnestly. "*Look,*" he said to Trevor, "I promise you won't be involved!"

Clayton was amazed. There was Todd, pleading. It didn't suit him. Things were bad.

Todd continued: "But if you leave Barton now there *will* be grounds for suspicion. All I want is for you to stay put here, carry on as normal—"

"No chance!" Trevor declared.

Todd glanced bitterly at Trevor. "Don't you think you owe me something?"

"Just *what* exactly?"

"Who set you up in speedway?" enquired Todd.

"Your means to an end," Trevor told him. "You were out to clobber my old man. I was just a pawn."

"You never complained!"

"I was on to a good thing," said Trevor. "But so were *you,* Todd, so don't make it sound like you did me favours. And now I want *out!*"

Anger flashed across Todd's face. "All right," he shouted. "Then *get!*"

Trevor didn't move. "I need money," he said quietly.

Todd smiled. "Money?"

"I'm going to hole up in London till all this has blown over," Trevor explained anxiously. "I need some ready cash."

"But Trevor," said Todd, suddenly conscious of his new power, "I've paid you . . ."

"You promised the same again."

"That the only reason you came out here?" asked Todd. Trevor was silent. Todd gave a sarcastic smile. "You don't seriously expect me to help you?"

"I'm just collecting what you owe me, Todd!"

Todd glanced at him. "I'll pay you only if you agree to stick around and see things through." He watched Trevor carefully.

Trevor was silent for a moment. Then he nodded. "OK Todd. So long as you know what you're doing. I'll stay . . ."

Todd's laughter was harsh and bitter. "You're pretty easy to see through, Trevor. You've no intention of staying!" Trevor turned his back on Todd. "If you'd been straight about it, I might even have paid you."

"I've only had half what you promised!"

"Well, Trevor, that's fair," observed Todd. "I've received half your loyalty."

"*Right!*" Trevor went angrily to the cabin door and slid it open. He looked back at Todd, jabbing his finger at him. "If the law catches up with me, friend, I drop *you* straight in it!" Trevor stepped out on to the deck, sliding the door shut with a bang.

As Trevor emerged from the cabin and walked towards his motorbike, his every move was noted. Kerry was sitting astride his motorbike between the trees, watching. He had seen the three of them inside the cabin, and had seen enough to be sure that the discussion was not a friendly one. Now Trevor looked back angrily at the barge and then roared off down the track into the distance. Maybe that's the last time I will ever see Trev, thought Kerry, with deeply mixed feelings.

Inside the cabin, there was a moment's pause. "We're on our own, Clayton," said Todd quietly.

Clayton spoke tentatively but with the air of a man whose mind was made up: "I'm for pulling out, Todd," he said.

"Are you?"

Clayton looked uneasily at Todd, rubbing the edge of his chin with the tips of his fingers. "It's all gone too far, it's turned bad."

Todd looked Clayton over coldly. "The solar plexus was never your strong point."

"I came down to this dead-end hole against my better judgement!" he protested.

"Yes," recalled Todd, "you weren't entirely enthusiastic."

"I've gone along with everything, I've supported you throughout!"

"Not out of charity, Clayton – you've been paid something for it, I believe?"

"Not enough to risk gaol," Clayton said hotly.

"Very well then, Clayton – follow Trevor's example and *scram*!" Todd turned his back angrily on Clayton.

Clayton walked up to him. "Todd, look," he said. "You've built yourself out of nothing. From a country rough-neck into somebody to be reckoned with. And now – now your're tossing it all away over this vendetta with Hutson!"

Todd was stiff and tense. "I'm not giving this up."

"Accept it, Todd, you can't win," Clayton urged.

Todd shook his head firmly. "No. I've come home to Barton and here I intend to stay."

"What about the law?" asked Clayton.

"Let them come," said Todd fiercely. "If I fall, then I drag Hutson right down with me."

"Todd, it's never worth it!"

"That's for me to decide."

Clayton couldn't comprehend Todd's attitude. "You're out of your mind!"

"Whatever happens," Todd said with finality, "I intend to see Hutson ruined."

It hadn't worked. Todd hadn't swallowed the bait, Kerry decided. An hour had passed since Trevor left the barge. Kerry knew that he had to do something drastic. But *what?* He gripped the handlebars and hunched himself over the motorbike, looking up and down the canal. Then Kerry spotted the fishermen on the far bank by the canal locks. An idea suddenly struck him. It would be taking a crazy risk. But he saw no way out of it. He braced himself and made the first decisive move.

Kerry kicked the starting-pedal and wove his way down between the trees towards the canal track. He roared out through the ferns on to the gravel and pulled up beside Todd's barge, keeping the motorbike engine running.

He suddenly started shouting at the top of his voice: "*Edwards! Todd Edwards!* Do you hear me, *Edwards!*"

Todd's eyes shot across to the cabin window. He saw Kerry on the canal track. He was shouting at him!

"Has Trevor gone and told you all about it, Edwards?" came Kerry's voice. "Did Trevor tell you? The law are on the way!"

"It's him," said Clayton in a bewildered voice. "It's Hutson's kid!"

"He must've been out there all the time," Todd said, "watching!"

Kerry's display had attracted the attention of the fishermen. Some of them stood, leaving their rods, and began walking past the canal locks, along the bank towards the canal track.

Kerry kept up his bombardment: "You made a bad mistake there, Edwards, abducting my girlfriend! Because she and her parents have gone down to Barton police station and they're making a complaint against you!"

The cabin door was suddenly slid back and Todd stepped angrily out on to the deck. Kerry felt the sweat prickling the back of his neck but he kept on shouting: "So you'd better get out quick, mate, while you've still got the chance. Otherwise you and your fat friend there will end up sewing mailbags!"

Todd's face was pinched with fury. He crossed the deck to the side of the barge. "*Right!*"

Clayton remained behind the cabin doorway. "Cool it, Todd!" he whispered.

"What's going on there?" one of the fishermen shouted over from the bank.

Kerry glanced across. "Do these people know who you are, Edwards?" Then, his arm outstretched, Kerry pointed the finger at Todd. "His name is Todd Edwards! A gangster from the London underworld! Extortion, blackmail, bribery – that's his line!

Todd clambered off the side of the barge and glared at Kerry, his face red and taut. "*You!*" he hissed.

"It's all over, Edwards," said Kerry coldly.

"Todd . . ." Clayton called from inside the cabin.

"You're *finished*," Kerry spat.

Todd pointed his fist. His voice was choked with rage. "*You* – you're going to fetch it!" He suddenly rushed at Kerry, running towards him across the gravel.

Kerry quickly revved up the motorbike, twisted it round and went tearing off down the track.

Todd raced to the Maxi, clambered in and fired the starter.

"Todd, *stop!*" Clayton shouted from the cabin doorway.

Kerry roared away at high speed down the track. Todd put

the vehicle into gear, and the car pitched forward, zooming down the track after Kerry.

Kerry careered past the group of fishermen, who stood as if stunned. Kerry gave a quick, anxious glance behind at the pursuing car. It was a short distance behind, rapidly advancing upon him.

Again Kerry looked round to see the car right behind, only a few feet away from his back wheel. He then began riding the machine in a zig-zag direction across the track, in an attempt to confuse Todd. Suddenly there came a loud horn blast from the car, Todd's reply to Kerry's manoeuvre.

Todd watched intently through the windscreen. He began thumping violently on the horn, then he pressed his fist down and kept it there, producing a long, continuous moan. He saw Kerry swing the bike in towards the woodland side of the track. He changed gear and the car took the corner with a screech, following Kerry along the path. Kerry's bike bounced over the rough uneven track and the car followed, tyres screeching as Todd cornered wildly.

Back on the barge, Clayton had not been idle. He had gathered some clothes and the protection money and rammed it all into a grip. Suddenly he heard the wail of a police siren. Crouching low, he peered through the cabin window.

A motorbike rider lead a big white police car along the track. The fishermen had congregated in a group near the barge. The leading rider, wearing a black helmet, goggles and a long black trench coat, pulled up to talk to the fishermen. One of the fishermen pointed down the track.

The black rider swung his bike round, and signalled to the police car as he bounded down the track. The police car followed, siren wailing, emergency roof light flashing intermittently.

Clayton sighed with relief. No one had realised that he remained on the barge. He peered through the window to make sure that all was clear. Then he picked up the grip and stepped out on to the deck. He heaved himself up the bank, and started hurrying in the opposite direction.

Todd was tensely poised over the steering wheel, Kerry

roared along the path ahead. Suddenly, through the windscreen, Todd saw Kerry force his bike off the path, tearing along beside the old gravel workings. Todd violently changed gear. The Maxi bounced off the path and ploughed its way after Kerry. The sound of the police car siren came swelling up behind them.

Kerry negotiated the bike through a clutch of trees, impassible for the Maxi. But Todd swung the car forward, swerving out beyond the trees, heading Kerry off.

Kerry met the car as he emerged from the trees and swung the bike down the steep slope of an old gravel pit to avoid collision. There was an ugly squeal as his bike skidded on the dusty surface. Kerry tumbled off, and rolled away across the ground. He picked himself up and ran desperately across the track, but Todd had come round the end of the pit and now pitched the car forward, right after Kerry.

The police car siren whined loudly from nearby. Lead by the black motorbike rider, the police vehicle swung across the heathland. The rider spotted Kerry running in the sights of the Maxi and suddenly tore forward.

Kerry ran down the sloping heath, desperately trying to wrench the helmet from his head. Todd closed in behind, and levelled the car at Kerry, all set to run him into the ground.

Suddenly Kerry leaped to one side, darting out of the track of the car, rolling over, head over heels, winding himself in a ball across the ground.

Todd braked. He backed the car and redirected it towards Kerry, moving swiftly towards him. The black motorbike rider suddenly swung into Todd's path and roared up towards him.

Todd wrenched the steering wheel violently to avoid the rider. He swung the Maxi away, and pitched forward, past the black rider. Then Todd saw it. Lying fifteen yards away. The huge, hungry, jagged shape of the gravel pit looked up at him like the mouth of a killer shark. Todd turned as stiff as a robot. He forced his foot to the brake pedal and jammed it down. The brakes screeched in an ugly howl and the Maxi slid towards the edge of the pit. Todd opened his mouth to scream, but no sound came. The car plunged into the pit. There was a huge explosion like a bomb going off. And then silence.

Two constables climbed out of the police car and ran over. Then they stood there, at the edge of the pit, shaking their heads hopelessly.

Kerry picked himself up from the ground. He was shaking. Then the motorbike rider sped over to him. That cop had saved his life. He drew up beside Kerry, unstrapped his helmet and pulled off his goggles. Then Kerry realised that the rider wasn't a police motorcyclist. It was Dad.

Richard Hutson had taken Nikki home before he contacted the police. Now she was waiting on the front steps, looking anxiously up and down the road. As the police car pulled up, she ran down to meet it.

Kerry climbed out of the car, and limply crossed the pavement to Nikki. He looked pale and shaken. "It's all over," he said to her in a drained, exhausted voice. "Todd . . . Todd's dead . . ."

12 King Kerry

A few days later, Kerry and Nikki were leaning over the rail of the harbour wall, overlooking the sea. It was the first time they had seen each other since the aftermath of the violence at the canal. Kerry had been busy answering police questions and attending the inquest on Todd.

They sat in silence for a while, watching the boats bob up and down on the green stretch of water. Then Nikki asked: "Anything more been heard of Trevor?"

Kerry shook his head. "Nope. He's got out of Barton for good, I reckon," he said quietly.

"How's your Dad taken it?"

Kerry frowned. He looked worried. "Pretty badly. He wanted to make a public statement."

"Statement?"

"Yeah," explained Kerry. "So that people in Barton know the truth. All of it. What happened in the past. Sort of confession . . ."

"Nothing served by that," said Nikki. "Only hurt other people."

"Most of all himself. I talked him out of it. He won't make a statement now." Kerry looked across the water. "Got to live with it by himself . . ."

There was a pause. Nikki asked: "Nothing more about Todd's sidekick?"

"The police never caught up with him," Kerry told her. "Nobody's interested in Clayton now they've had the inquest on Todd and the case has been closed. The police have shelved the whole thing."

"Best forgotten anyway," Nikki said.

Kerry looked at her. "Funny," he said, "know it sounds daft, but looking back on it, it's like none of it really happened to me. But to somebody else. Somebody different. Know what I mean?"

"Yeah . . ."

"Weird, ain't it? . . ." Kerry suddenly got up. They were both brooding too much. "Come on," he said, "let's go home and have some tea."

They walked down the pavement to Kerry's motorbike. Kerry looked at Nikki and grinned. "Coming to speedway Sunday afternoon, then?"

Nikki gave him a jaundiced look. "Never give up, do you?"

"*The Barons* have got a new rider," Kerry said with a smile.

But Nikki couldn't have cared less. "*Wow!*"

"Three guesses who . . ."

"You mean they've gone and picked *you*?" Nikki sounded quite amazed.

"Yeah," Kerry told her, "matter of fact they have."

"Thought the whole idea of speedway was to win!"

Kerry mounted the motorbike. "Ha ha, very funny, we'll let you know," he said lightly.

"Now I know why you paid for the ice-creams!"

"You don't have to come on Sunday."

"Is that a fact?" said Nikki archly. "What they pick you for?"

"Maybe they thought I'd be some good."

"Streuth," said Nikki, "they *must* be hard up!"

Kerry smiled at her blandly. Nikki looked irritated. "Why aren't you getting narked?" she asked.

Kerry shrugged. "Life's too short."

Nikki grinned. She climbed on to the pillion and clung to Kerry. "Hey," she said, "bags secretary of your fan club!"

Nikki gripped the wire-netting behind the barricade of the standing-room area and looked out across the deserted speedway track. Racing was due to start in a few minute's time. Someone tapped Nikki on the shoulder. She glanced round. It was Kerry's father. "Wotchyer!" grinned Nikki.

He had a couple of hot-dogs and handed one to Nikki. "Here Nikki – for you." Richard Hutson sounded a bit nervous.

"Ta!" said Nikki.

He looked out across the track, feeling a bit self-conscious. It was many years since he had been to Barton Stadium. "Had a job finding you," he murmured.

"Kerry know you're coming this afternoon?"

Hutson shook his head, smiling. "Don't tell him, or I'll never live it down!"

"Might spot you stood here!" Nikki suggested.

He shook his head knowingly. "You've never ridden in the speedway, Nikki . . ."

Nikki took another bite out of her hot-dog. "No, that's true," said Nikki wryly.

"Good heavens!" grinned Hutson. He was looking towards the main gate.

Nikki glanced round. "What?"

"Old Nulty . . ."

Nulty, leaning on his stick, limped into the stadium. He stood among the crowd, blinking, looking a bit confused by all the bustle and noise. Then he spotted Hutson by the standing-room area, waving him over, and limped across.

Kerry sat astride his motorbike in the pits. He was wearing a brand-new tunic and pulled on a helmet decked out in Barton colours.

Tom walked up to him, grinning. He nodded at Kerry's new outfit. "All right, then?"

Kerry self-consciously pulled at his front tunic, straightening it. "It's so stiff and awkward," he complained, "like a new suit!"

"A good dose of sweat and mud will soon break that outfit in!" laughed Tom.

Kerry grinned, strapping up his helmet. "Yeah!"

"Glad you're riding with us, Kerry," Tom said. "Best of luck . . ."

"Thanks, Tom . . ."

"Nervous?"

"Dead scared!" Kerry admitted.

Tom grinned. "Good," said the new captain of *The Barons*. "You'll do fine . . ."

"*Here he comes!*" cried Nikki, pointing towards the track as four speedway riders emerged from the pits. Kerry rode on the outside lane. The surrounding crowds let out a wild cheer as the riders approached the grids.

The loudspeakers crackled and the announcer said: ". . . . home meeting between *The Barons* of Barton . . . and *The Hawks* of Homefield . . . riding for *The Barons* . . . their captain, Tom Arnold . . ."

Kerry crouched over his motorbike behind the starting tapes, and heard his name announced over the loudspeakers: ". . . young Kerry Hutson . . . riding here in his first track meeting . . . good luck there, Kerry . . . !"

Kerry began revving up his engine as the loudspeaker announcements were concluded. The four riders were poised behind the tapes. Tom gave Kerry a thumbs-up sign.

The tapes suddenly shot up and the riders roared forward. A wild cheer went up from the crowds.

"*They're off!*" said Richard Hutson, his eyes fixed intently on Kerry. Nikki gripped the wire-netting and shouted for Kerry. Nulty stood there, propped against his stick, quietly watching the race.

Kerry swept forward, poised over the motorbike, cruising swiftly down the track, the shale dust swirling around him.